THE GREATNESS CHAIR SOLUTION

A Guidebook to Successful Parenting and Teaching

Kathleen Devorah Friend M.D

© 2021 by Kathleen Devorah Friend M.D. All rights reserved.
Words Matter Publishing
P.O. Box 531
Salem, Il 62881
www.wordsmatterpublishing.com

No part of this publication may be reproduced, stored in a retrieval system, or transmitted in any way by any means—electronic, mechanical, photocopy, recording, or otherwise—without the prior permission of the copyright holder, except as provided by USA copyright law.

ISBN: 978-1-953912-50-3

Library of Congress Catalog Card Number: 2021952838

Dedicated to all children and their grownups to bring greater love, harmony and beauty to our global village.

ACKNOWLEDGEMENTS

As anyone who has written a book knows, there are far too many people to acknowledge in a few paragraphs. I can honestly say, everyone in my life experience has contributed to the creation of this book. I stand on the shoulders of so many others and can only hope this all-inclusive thank-you registers somewhere in the hearts of those who have crossed my path.

There are those who stand out and have provided inspiration, support, encouragement and a patient ear. I want to thank my publisher Tammy Koelling of Words Matter Publishing for tireless encouragement, vision and support. Without her, this book would not have come to fruition. I also want to personally thank my husband and son for honest challenging of my ideas which helps me sharpen my concepts. I am indebted to Susanna and Puran Bair for introducing me to heart rhythm meditation and helping me see my greatness so I could make my unique contributions to the world. Without their guidance, I would not have embarked on the path of writing. I am also grateful for the support of two pivotal communities - IAM Heart and the Nurtured Heart Approach trainers. And lastly, to Marcie Towle, an advanced trainer for the Nurtured Heart Approach and Amanda Rayne who volunteered hours of time to provide invaluable input and editing that improved the structure and clarity of the book's message.

TABLE OF CONTENTS

RAISING THE CURTAIN 1

SETTING THE STAGE: THE FIVE W'S 9
- WHY 11
- WHO 17
- WHAT 20
- WHEN 24
- WHERE 25

INTRODUCTION TO THE SEVEN-WEEK PLAN 27

WEEK ONE: INTENTION 29
- INTENTION 29
- ACTIVITIES FOR YOU 34
- ACTIVITIES WITH THE KIDS 38

WEEK TWO: ATTENTION 39
- ATTENTION 39
- ACTIVITIES FOR YOU 46
- ACTIVITIES WITH THE KIDS 48

WEEK THREE: POSTURE 51
- POSTURE 51
- ACTIVITIES FOR YOU 56
- ACTIVITIES WITH THE KIDS 57

WEEK FOUR: SENSATION — 59
SENSATION — 59
ACTIVITIES FOR YOU — 71
ACTIVITIES WITH THE KIDS — 73

WEEK FIVE: INSPIRATION — 77
INSPIRATION — 77
ACTIVITIES FOR YOU — 82
ACTIVITIES WITH THE KIDS — 84

WEEK SIX: INVOCATION — 85
INVOCATION — 85
ACTIVITIES FOR YOU — 91
100 GREATNESS WORDS — 93
ACTIVITIES WITH KIDS — 95

WEEK SEVEN: PUTTING IT ALL TOGETHER IN THE GREATNESS CHAIR. — 97
PUTTING IT ALL TOGETHER IN THE GREATNESS CHAIR — 97
ACTIVITIES FOR YOU — 102
ACTIVITIES WITH KIDS — 103

WEEK EIGHT: RECAP AND NEXT STEPS — 107

APPENDIX A: STEPS OF HEART RHYTHM MEDITATION — 109

APPENDIX B: SOCIAL EMOTIONAL LEARNING (SEL) AND THE CASEL FRAMEWORK FOR SCHOOLS — 111

APPENDIX C: DIMENSIONS OF WELL-BEING – RICHARD DAVIDSON PH.D., ET. AL. — 119

RESOURCES — 121

ABOUT THE AUTHOR — 123

RAISING THE CURTAIN

"To be admitted to Nature's hearth costs nothing. None is excluded, but excludes himself. You only have to push aside the curtain."
- Henry David Thoreau

"There's something in life that's a curtain and I keep trying to raise it."
- Maxine Hong Kingston.

Welcome to the Greatness Chair Workbook, where we will sharpen our abilities to find and nurture the inherent greatness in the children we parent and teach. If you are reading this book, I can assume you have the same desire to bring out the best in children! How we go about it matters. I offer a novel approach to the subject where we learn to integrate our hearts AND minds to accomplish this task. As an adult and child psychiatrist with close to thirty years of clinical experience and ten years of experience practicing heart rhythm meditation, I am ready to share the synthesis of my life's work and experience with you in this book.

As quoted above, Henry David Thoreau, the American poet, essayist and philosopher, understood the value of observing nature. He identified the need to pause, reflect and allow truth to reveal itself behind the curtain. Chinese-American novelist Maxine Hong Kingston, also quoted above, mentioned tapping into our desire to "build a better mousetrap" when she refers to her continuous attempts to raise the curtain.

My aim in writing this book is to help you raise the curtain to reveal the truth of the child in your life. We owe it to the children to see behind the curtain of misbehavior, tantrums and the assortment of other challenges they bring. We are challenged to keep "raising the curtain" to fulfill both our dreams and wishes for ourselves and those of the children we care for.

We want to find the greatness in the child that is already present and help it develop. The skills to accomplish this can be learned. You will be guided through a seven-week process to develop your abilities to see yourself and the children more clearly and to implement strategies to help them prosper. You will learn how to use six powers to access your heart and learn how to integrate your heart with your mind. These steps are powerful allies to help us and children succeed.

Based on my clinical experience, techniques work best in the context of strong relationships. Many parenting and teaching techniques fail because they are not sufficiently built on the foundation of a safe, nurturing and connected relationship. The techniques presented in this book both build on your current relationship with the child and also teach you to create a deeper connection with them.

Have I have stimulated your curiosity, imagination or ideals in these first few paragraphs? If the answer is yes, I know a lot of things about you already! You are passionate about children and are open to new ways of bringing out the best in them. At times you will feel lost, unsure of yourself, and may question the power of the techniques in this book. My basic premises in this book may seem overly idealistic and Pollyannaish (Pollyanna was a character in a book of the same title, who always saw the best in every situation). All of us have a storehouse of knowledge, wisdom and experience and I want to honor that. I suggest you approach this program with a clean slate for the sake of curiosity and experimentation. Later there will be time to go back and creatively weave in your own wisdom, ideas and methods. Perhaps you will write me and tell me what works better! No one has all the answers, but I have found great power in using the Greatness Chair in my medical practice and have been witness to rapid changes experienced by others who have tried this method.

This book is for parents, teachers, coaches, grandparents, therapists and anyone who has an interest in guiding the next generation, or has frequent contact with them. As an adult, you can also use this approach to re-parent your own inner child.

The Greatness Chair was born out of my experience with the Nurtured Heart Approach® (NHA) developed by Howard Glasser years ago to deal with intense children who did not respond to conventional methods. Although this book does not lay out that full method, which is covered expertly in other sources, it rests firmly in the approach.

I initially wanted to implement the full NHA approach and training where I worked as a child psychiatrist, but I felt blocked at every turn! At first, I was disappointed and discouraged, but then I took matters into my own hands. My children's books, *The*

Greatness Chair and *Sarah in the Greatness Chair,* as well as this book, are my creative work-arounds. Truly, necessity was the mother of invention! Shifting to book writing instead of in-person training or therapy to deliver the message I believed would help the families I treated was an important lesson and life-altering event for me. I discovered latent qualities of greatness in myself that were the keys to fulfilling my heart's wish to bring out the best in children. I hope my journey will inspire you to discover qualities of greatness in yourself that are secretly clamoring for an opportunity to manifest.

We cannot afford to continue seeing ourselves and children through a narrow window of cultural and societal expectations. The children are not flourishing and rates of ADHD, autism, developmental and behavioral issues, depression, anxiety and suicide tell a sobering story. According to the National Center for Health Statistics, one in every 5-6 children have mental health concerns and suicide is the second leading cause of death in children between the ages of 10 and 14. Prevalence data from the annual reports of the non-profit organization Mental Health of America (MHA) indicates yearly rising rates of depression and suicidal ideation. In the 2020 MHA report, 13% of youth aged 12-17 reported at least one episode of major depression in the past year, compared to 12.6% in 2019. MHA data collected from September of 2020, during the COVID-19 pandemic, found over half of eleven to seventeen-year-old youth reported having thoughts of suicide or self-harm more than half the days or nearly every day for the two weeks prior to the survey. Hospital admissions for adolescents with suicidal ideation has skyrocketed as well. Boston Children's Hospital reported a 47% increase in admissions for suicidal ideation or attempts during the same time period (July-October) in 2020 compared to 2019. The availability of mental health services for children varies across the country but there are widespread shortages of appropriately-trained providers and lack of accessibility is commonplace.

Teachers and parents are often hemmed into a rigid set of expectations for children, dictated by educational systems or from their fears of deviating too far from the "script", lest the child be unable to succeed in our 21st-century competitive world, regardless of whether this aligns with their own ideals. These fears are based in reality and a wise parent and educator should not be completely dismissive of the external circumstances our children face that are unique to our current time and place in history. Yet we each have a unique path through life and bring our own distinctive brand of genius. The more we understand children and ourselves from this perspective, the more successful we are at navigating life. Our children learn to see themselves through our eyes. We have the ability to "refocus" what we see to reflect back a version worth growing into. Bringing one's individual gifts to life breeds success which is affirming, healthy and potent.

I want to clarify that the greatness concept is not a sugarcoating of reality. It is about the truth of the moment. It is optimism with open eyes. It is about using our attention to focus on what is going right instead of the problems. And magically, problems lessen. Our aim is to see who our children are and nurture that. Just as we all have a unique fingerprint, we each have a unique constellation of greatness. We can help children learn to see that in themselves and bring their special gifts and talents to the table.

Let me take you on a journey to discover the unique music of each child and help them sing their song. And along the way, I wish the same for you.

Each week you will be guided through one of the six basic powers: **intention, attention, posture, sensation, inspiration and invocation**, with suggested activities for you and the children to learn new skills which reinforce the concept. In the final week, we will put it all together in the Greatness Chair! These six powers were originally conceived by Susanna and Puran Bair of IAM Heart to teach heart rhythm meditation. In this book, we will use the six powers to both teach heart rhythm meditation, and amplify our social-emotional skill set.

We need to learn how to use the six powers to manage ourselves in order for us to be most effective with the children. This can be a hard pill to swallow - that we must change ourselves to help our children. I think most parents and teachers understand this concept intellectually, but emotionally it can feel like a kick in the gut and may trigger feelings of inadequacy, guilt or shame. Let me assure you, the need to make changes says nothing about how good of a parent or teacher you already are, but parenting and guiding children in today's world needs to be notched up. Given the current state of our world, it is apparent to many of us that we need to step up our game to create an enduring and sustainable future. We cannot do this from inner self-poverty. We need the energetic and emotional riches of a strong heart to do this work. The world truly needs the unique contribution of everyone.

The book is best implemented in the order presented for full impact. Although people began with the Greatness Chair right away, and many reported surprisingly profound results, the experience will be richer and the results more far-reaching following the seven-week program from beginning to end. Think of this as an adventure in slow cooking instead of fast food. Savor the journey, slow down and enjoy the ride.

To your greatness growing!

SETTING THE STAGE: THE FIVE W'S

"The kids who need the most love will ask for it in the most unloving ways."
-- **Anonymous**

"Inner Wealth™ is a resource available to even the poorest family."
-- **M. Towle.**

WHY

The mental health of our children is floundering. In the Introduction, I presented the sobering statistic that, according to the National Center for Health Statistics, one in every 5-6 children has a mental or developmental issue of significance. The rates of childhood anxiety, ADHD, autism, learning disabilities, developmental delays and depression are high - and rising. The number of children on psychotropic medication is staggering. Exact numbers are hard to come by, but the use of medication is widely prevalent in the United States and often is the first-line solution. As a child psychiatrist, I have been all too aware of this practice and have medicated children myself during my career. My purpose in writing this book is to make this scenario less likely for your children or students. Medication has a place for some children and this should not be regarded as shameful or as a failure. My training as a child psychiatrist advocates for therapy and a behavioral approach as the first step in treatment, but frequently parents and teachers give up on non-pharmacologic strategies too quickly. I am sympathetic to the roadblocks that occur in the pursuit of non-medication alternatives which can result from ineffective services and programs with inadequate know-how, resources, time or support for implementation. Many parents tell me they do not want to medicate their children but feel at a loss when it comes to alternatives. Even if considerable time and investment have been made on the part of the teacher or parent, there will be children who benefit from medication for mental health issues. We can draw a parallel to the diabetic who follows a healthy lifestyle of exercise, weight loss and an appropriate diet, yet still needs medication to control blood sugar.

The reasons for the rising mental health issues in children are multifactorial and complex, but some notable contributors include poverty, poor nutrition with an excess of processed food, stressed parents and teachers, educational performance demands imposed by national standards with relentless testing, social isolation imposed by the COVID-19 pandemic, social media bullying, excessive screen time, inadequate amounts of physical activity, and gutting the arts from school curriculum. You may be able to add to this list based on your own experience.

Children have always lived in a world where they and their parents had to navigate storms of adversity. Throughout history, many individuals thrived and rose to greatness in the face of these hardships. Today, children seem to have less ability to bounce back and deal with adversity. The reasons for that are complex and beyond the scope of this book, but building inner emotional wealth by helping our children see and discover their unique greatness is a powerful antidote to help them weather adverse childhood experiences. I want to help you build optimism, emotional strength, and resilience in both yourself and the children in your life.

Many children have an inner portfolio of deficiencies and problems rather than strengths. In other words, they experience themselves as flawed. We can contribute to this as parents and teachers so easily and innocently despite great intentions! I want to help you become artists with the ability to create beauty inside yourself and the children so these inner portfolios contain masterpieces.

I want to share my personal why for writing this book. In a flash of honesty with myself during a session with a family, I realized I could not listen to **one more parent** tell me everything that was going wrong with their child. I felt like I was listening to a rap sheet of badness. Naturally, the child would not want to be present in the appointment and would slump in the chair and avoid eye contact. Responses to my questions might be grunts, if anything at all.

However, I understood the parent completely. They brought their child to me because something was wrong and they wanted my help to fix the problem. Isn't that what they were supposed to do? It made sense to me, until it didn't. So, I decided to try something new. The Greatness Chair was born.

When I started putting children in a simple chair next to my desk and asked them to tell me about their greatness, things started to change. Suddenly they looked at me - often confused but interested. Some children readily shared a greatness and others needed to be shown the greatness they were exhibiting right in that moment in my office. For example, if they were having trouble finding a greatness quality, I commented on their greatness of trying hard and their cooperation even though they didn't know how to answer my question. I followed each kid like a hawk and found greatness in everything they were showing me. This got their attention and smiles. Parents' faces lit up and they wanted to jump in and tell me more about their child's positive qualities. What parent really wants to focus on the bad stuff? They were only too happy and excited to have the opportunity to share the strengths of their children. This enabled us to approach the problems they were having in an atmosphere of safety, positivity and hope and the child was less likely to feel blame or shame when the difficulties were discussed.

Common Struggles for Parents and Teachers

Another reason I am writing this book is to help parents and teachers with common pitfalls which derail their good intentions: wanting to be the child's friend; inability to self-regulate their own emotional states; teacher burnout; and overly rigid and inflexible administrative policies in schools. Let's look at each of these pitfalls more closely.

Many adults say, "I want to be my/the child's friend." They are rejecting the old-fashioned authoritarian model of "parent or teacher knows best" but then may become overly permissive and abdicate the necessary role of guiding with clarity of values and intentions when the line is crossed. We hope our children feel the acceptance, closeness, and safety they feel with friends, but children need guidance and it is not an even playing field as they require direction from a trusted leader who has the ability to set goals using clear values. Working through the weekly activities in this book to clarify your goals and values, from the point of view of both mind and heart, will enhance your ability to be an effective leader.

In the school environment, I see the difficulty not so much as teachers being unwilling to set clear expectations and rules, but as teachers who operate within the larger context of their school districts that are overly authoritarian with rigid expectations, strict inflexible rules and policies, and an expectation of obedience over independence. I have witnessed a decrease in tolerance for children's behaviors in the school setting at all grade levels. Even preschoolers are "suspended" or "kicked out" for aggressive or generally non-compliant behaviors. This pattern disproportionately affects black and Hispanic students. In 2020 the ACLU reported that black preschool children are 3.6 times more likely than white children to receive one or more out of school suspensions. As children age, the disparity continues and is even greater for black females, who are up against not only racial bias but rigid gender expectations of appropriate "girl" behaviors. Black females are 5.5 times more likely to be suspended from school from kindergarten through 12th grade.

Aggression in schools is not new and, despite the widely publicized incidents of mass shootings in recent years, statistics reported by the National Center for Education Statistics actually show a downward trend in violent crime statistics. This is no comfort for children who continue to be victimized, nor for the children who are increasingly funneled out of the public-school system into the criminal justice system - the "school to prison pipeline". Despite the fact that children's behaviors at school reflect multiple influences both within and out of school, I believe that using the precepts in this book will help decrease aggression in the classroom and increase the likelihood of school success. Although the ideal situation is continuity of these practices between home and school, the teacher can still have a profound effect on the classroom milieu despite lack of control over administrative policies or parental participation. The ideas in this book are free and empowering and require no administrative permission!

Teacher burnout is prevalent and results in disengagement with the children. Teachers are underpaid and undervalued with inadequate resources and support to manage the special needs of many of the children in their classrooms. The 2015-2016 data from the University of Pennsylvania Graduate School of Education indicated that 40% of new teachers leave the profession within the first five years. Since the COVID-19 pandemic, even greater numbers of new and seasoned teachers are considering quitting.

Another significant challenge I see well-meaning parents and teachers encounter is that of self-regulation when dealing with a child who is out of control. The adult becomes triggered and cannot calm their nervous system sufficiently to co-regulate the child. Most of us were not taught these skills as children and we will need to learn this skill along with the children. No shame or blame here. I believe we all do better when we know better, and the program outlined in this book is designed to give adults the tools needed to begin self-regulation.

I want to share a story written by a mom who struggled with self-regulation during a challenging situation with her son but turned things around later with the concepts of the Greatness Chair.

I had to share a story about your book today. It was beyond touching. I am a crier and I'm so touched I can't even cry about it.

So today my son, E-, took this Lego tiger with him to the store next door. We walked over with his bike and toy in one hand. I saw the toy after I left, and told him he shouldn't have brought it as it will get lost or broken....

I got to the store, and went to the bathroom. When I returned, my son is pointing at his toy with no tail or leg any more, and whimpering. I LOST it. I YELLED AT HIM all across every aisle I could walk through. I was so livid. I often tell him not to take his toys places and this particular toy I love and he LOVED... I screamed at him in front of everyone, I couldn't have cared less. I got home and complained to my husband. I was livid all DAY and man was that silly....

Then he and I do our bed time routine, and he picks the book he wants to read, and he picks The Greatness Chair. As I'm reading, I'm holding my breath and see how well the book fits into the day, and how emotionally intelligent he is, far beyond my awareness or comprehension. After finishing the book, we revisited and reframed the day. Him bringing his toys were a sign of his love for them and how he had wanted to share an adventure with them. I reframed my screaming at him as a sign of my love for him. When we finished, I was filled with a sense of such strength and fullness, and a feeling beyond tears. I just had to share your book's effect on me and my emotionally intelligent son. I must have gotten something right because emotional intelligence is something I try to teach him despite not modeling it well. I'm completely floored.

Thank you so much for writing your book. It's helping everyone survive.

Who

Who is this book for? Simply put - parents and teachers of all types, children of all ages, and adults with inner children! This includes bio parents, blended families with stepchildren, grandparents raising children, foster and adoptive families, and same-sex marriages and partnerships raising children. I believe the basic principles outlined in this book transcend socioeconomic status, gender, race and culture. I invite readers to find creative ways to integrate this approach within the understanding of their own background. This is built into the approach during the clarification of your values and desired outcomes in Week One.

The potential benefits are for families, classrooms and the world at large. When children are filled with emotional strength and connection, the ripples are exponential. I am certainly not alone in my belief that the future rests with the children. We all have a sense of the importance of this issue but can get overwhelmed and discouraged because the job is hard and can seem hopeless at times. Children don't come with an instruction manual.

Let's look at several different types of children to see how the Greatness Chair can apply to diverse ages and circumstances. Names have been altered in these examples for confidentiality.

Jay is an intense seven-year-old. His mom read my book The Greatness Chair to him and they had fun drawing greatness chairs of their own. Mom used the approach for a few days and then forgot and returned to her usual nagging and whining. One night in an intense moment when Mom was yelling at him yet again to go take a shower, Jay slammed the shower door and it shattered all over the floor. Mom initially became more enraged but then shifted to feel concern for him and the small cut on his foot. Once she calmed, she asked him if he had a bad day like the little boy in my Greatness Chair book and he nodded. So, Mom then asked, "What do you think your greatness was?" Imagine saying that after your child was so out of control that they shattered the shower door! He answered, "I'm strong." They went on to identify other greatness qualities and left it there. Later that night, Jay apologized for breaking the door and Mom said, "You have the courage to admit your mistakes." Mom then apologized for being overly critical. They both felt better, and Mom is now determined to keep the energy right-side up!

A teenage boy in my practice with multiple disadvantages in life, including cognitive challenges, severe mood instability, poverty, family disruption, and parental mental illness seemed to enjoy the Greatness Chair activity even though I thought he might think it too juvenile. Absolutely not! One day I had to cancel his appointment. He was quite upset, and mentioned to the scheduler that he was looking forward to sitting in the Greatness Chair to tell me all the positive things he had accomplished in the past month.

It is amazing how small seeds can flourish into such beauty. Nature understands this truth and operates on it across all living things.

Teenagers can present a unique set of challenges in attempts to implement this model, but with modifications it is just as powerful. Teenagers are developmentally forming their own identities on their journey towards adulthood, and seeking independence from parents' opinions and rules. A typical teenager might reject reflections of greatness by the parent with sarcasm, rolled eyes, and apparent rejection. Teachers have an advantage in this age group because the task of individuation is from the parent, not all adults. Teenagers often welcome someone from outside the family showing a warm interest in them. With a teenager, the parent often has to work harder internally to exhibit more external restraint than is necessary for younger children. We want the teenager to sense our reset, our energy shift, while we hold the vision of greatness for them internally. This is not to say we give up on verbalizing the greatness we see in them, but we may have to be more selective about when and how much.

I will offer some modifications for the use of the Greatness Chair with teenagers who push back in Chapter Seven.

What

Here is the million-dollar question: Why do we need another parenting approach? There are many approaches to parenting and no shortage of advice from family members, therapists, psychologists, child psychiatrists, pediatricians and parent coaches with a range of experiences and insights. What I see missing is an understanding of how energy works and how to direct the flow of that energy in the desired direction. When we understand how energy flows from our hearts, we are empowered to create the family and classroom we dreamed of when we first decided to become a parent or teacher. This is not simply a new set of parenting techniques. Although I will be guiding you through a new skill set, the truth is that techniques alone mean very little unless they are embedded in a safe and connected relationship. As adults we steer the ship in the direction of our intentions for the children. But our effectiveness is embedded in connection. The ideas in this book will help form a connected, strong attachment to the child. As a result, behaviors change. No behavior chart can do that. No material reward will prove lasting or transforming. We may get short-term compliance, but the child will suffer in the long run. The energy from our hearts, combined with the Greatness Chair, will transform us and the children.

The aim of this book is to help you bring out the essence, the soul, of the child, and support their inherent design. When we have a seed and water it, it grows according to the template hidden inside. Some children are like roses, some fir trees, some magnolias and an endless variety of other possibilities. We all have built in greatness and we want to provide the conditions for its unfoldment.

There are strict rules of success in our achievement-oriented culture and it is hard not to compare children along those metrics. But success does not look the same for each child, and we can help them value their own gifts. When we focus on the greatness already occurring in the here and now, and expand our vocabulary to express it coupled with our heart's energy, we have a winning combination to build inner emotional wealth in the child.

Adding the Heart

This is a heart centered-approach. The heart is much more than a pump to circulate blood, nutrients and gases. It creates a powerful electromagnetic field produced by the electrical pulses we call heartbeats. The frequency, or rhythm, and strength of our heartbeats determine the size and power of the heart's electromagnetic field. Furthermore, our emotions change the rhythm and strength of our heartbeats through their direct effect on our autonomic nervous system and respiration rate. Therefore, our emotions have a direct impact on the heart's electromagnetic field. This is important because when I talk about using the power of our heart to make a difference for ourselves and children, I am in part referring to the changes in the heart field we produce with our emotions, which communicates wirelessly to those around us.

Although the heart contains many emotions, love is the main one we associate with the heart. It is also one of the most powerful. I have not met many parents or teachers who do not love children and want to operate from that place. But this energy of love needs to be directed appropriately or it ends up creating more problems for everyone.

Emotional Intelligence

There has been a recent emphasis in parent and teacher training to understand the emotions and reasons behind the child's behaviors as a way to both help them and to build a more secure and connected relationship. This empathetic and inquisitive approach is a well-intentioned and a positive step forward in raising and teaching children, but can easily backfire and throw gasoline on the fire. We do want to understand the child's feelings and motivations and help them learn to label and verbally express their inner states, but not in the heat of the moment! Otherwise, children can learn that misbehavior and distress is a sure-fire way to get love and attention.

Using the Greatness Chair elevates this approach to one where we give our energy to what is going right in a difficult situation while avoiding the pitfalls of showering our attention on misbehavior. I will teach you the value of resetting your own emotional state so that you may assist the child in resetting theirs. We are then able to empower the child with their own voice and give them the tools to discover their inner life more fully.

Alignment of the Greatness Chair with Contemporary Models of Parenting and Teaching

Support for the viewpoint in this book comes from research on parenting style and childhood outcomes later in life. Baumind and Maccoby (1983) described four parenting styles: authoritarian, authoritative, permissive and neglectful. Years of research into the outcomes of these parenting styles clearly supports the authoritative model, where the parent has high expectations which are firm and clear and occur in a context of parental responsiveness characterized by warmth and support. The program in this book fits into the authoritative style of parenting.

Lessons in the Greatness Chair aligns with Social Emotional Learning (SEL) programs being introduced in schools worldwide. This necessary addition to traditional academic education recognizes the importance of teaching emotional intelligence and social relatedness as a cornerstone to success and quality-of-life outcomes for children.

One of the major SEL frameworks called CASEL includes five broad categories of competencies: self-awareness, social awareness, self-management, relationship skills, and responsible decision-making. The model presented in this book helps with competencies in all five categories. By helping the child develop a healthy nervous system through adult co-regulation as discussed above, the child learns self-management which is the foundation for all the other CASEL competencies. In addition, when we mirror back to the child the greatness we observe, their sense of self and social awareness improves and is strength-based.

Richard Davidson, Ph.D., founder and director of the Center for Healthy Minds at the University of Wisconsin-Madison, has studied meditation and the emotional life of the brain for decades. Based on years of research, he developed a framework called the Model of Well-Being. The four categories of well-being, according to Davidson, are awareness, connection, insight and purpose. Although Davidson's model was not developed specifically for parents or educators, I recognize that the program outlined in this book aligns with these elements of well-being uncovered by years of scientific research. We will learn how to increase our attention and awareness and direct it in a way which leads to greater insights into children and ourselves. The shift of awareness from problems to greatness leads to deeper and more secure connections in relationships and helps children discover meaning and purpose in their lives related to their unique gifts. There is more information about CASEL and the Model of Well-Being in Appendix B and C for those who want to delve into this further.

When

The lessons in this book can be used anytime, but the use of the Greatness Chair is most impactful if it is set up as a routine at a specific time. Children love schedules and structure and we want to build excitement for the activity. Use of the Greatness Chair is also an effective way to start a therapy session and is useful during transitions or changes of routine. It is a powerful and quick way to hijack energy and turn it into a positive experience.

Where

You can implement the ideas behind the Greatness Chair anywhere you choose - in the classroom, in the home or during a therapy session. The possibilities are only limited by your imagination and the needs of the moment. The following personal experience illustrates a particularly creative implementation.

> *I was attending a Nurtured Heart Approach training and one of the participants was trying to figure out how to bring this approach to one of the foster families she was supporting, who was struggling with two teenagers. She read my children's book, The Greatness Chair, to them on the phone from a hotel room at the conference. The foster mom and both kids were in tears at the end. The therapist then asked each child to describe their greatness and without skipping a beat, they got it. The next day, the therapist received a phone call from the 17-year-old girl who, because of developmental delays, was on track to have a modified education but not a high school diploma. She asked for help to be placed somewhere where she could play out her greatness and get a better education and a real diploma. And this was from just having a book read to her!*

This therapist passionately and creatively worked within unusual circumstances to help bring out the greatness in these foster children. As a result, the children were deeply impacted and inspired to develop their own greatness!

Kids get this. They are ready to step into the best version of themselves if given a chance. We can guide them by putting the spotlight on what is already going right and baby-step them from their current condition into their full potential by teaching them about their greatness.

INTRODUCTION TO THE SEVEN-WEEK PLAN

Each week you will be guided through activities to strengthen one of the six basic powers. The six basic powers are **intention, attention, posture, sensation, inspiration and invocation.**

As the activities and skills build on one another, I strongly suggest you go through them in order. Each week you will be guided through activities to strengthen one of the six basic powers. There are activities for the adults and parallel activities focused on the children. The more preparation you do in the first six weeks, the more successful you will be when we finally pull out the Greatness Chair in Week Seven.

As mentioned previously, the biggest challenge I have seen is for adults to regulate their own reactions to children. Despite our best intentions, our nervous systems may become overloaded and then we yell, punish, or leave. In our quieter moments, we feel guilty and like failures. We promise to keep our cool next time and then the cycle repeats. Whether we blame ourselves or shift the blame to other adults close to the children, this cycle usually leaves us feeling powerless and defeated. Spending a few weeks on ourselves is the greatest gift we can give our students or children. We will make mistakes and have missteps along the way - we are human after all! But when we master our own ability to reset, then we can teach children how to reset into their next moment of greatness.

Materials needed:

1. A journal (Weeks 1-7)

2. A quiet place with a straight back chair (Weeks 1-7)

3. A copy of The Greatness Chair and Sarah in the Greatness Chair (Week 7).

WEEK ONE: INTENTION

Key concepts: conscious and subconscious beliefs, heart power, love, manifestation, values, wishes, mindset, desired outcomes, ideals

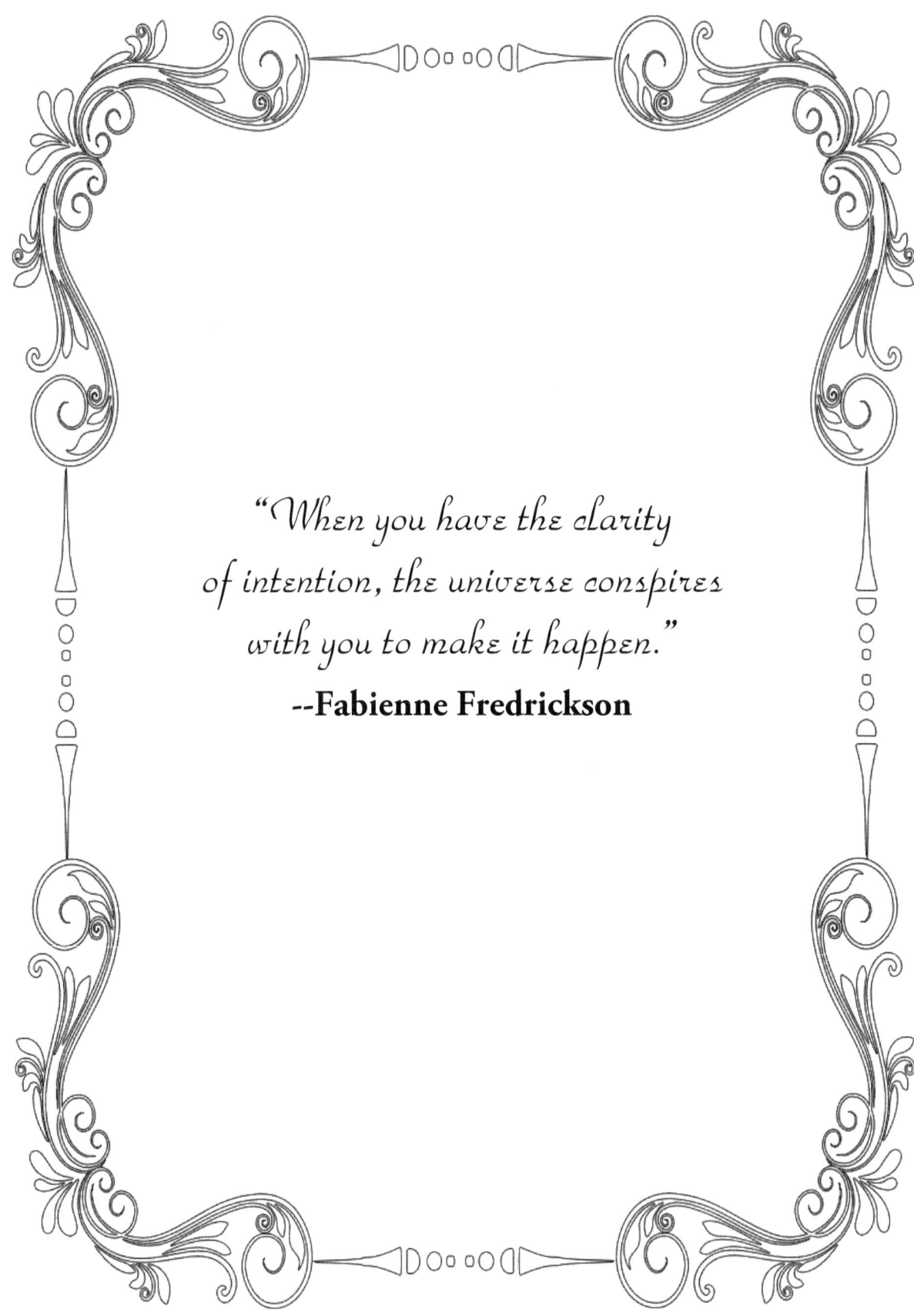

"When you have the clarity of intention, the universe conspires with you to make it happen."

--Fabienne Fredrickson

Intention is our desire and the outcome we wish to manifest.

Intention is intimately related to our purpose, beliefs, values, and ideals and it is linked closely to where we devote our time and energy.

Intention is the foundational piece for our success because, in tandem with emotion, it provides the primal energy for our actions and their outcomes. Dr. William Tiller, a physicist interested in psycho-energetics, carried out multiple experiments to understand the power of intention. He discovered that the connector between intention and manifestation was the emotional energy coming from a person's heart. Further research into the mechanism of intention by Rein and McCraty (1994) demonstrated that a subjects' intention to unravel DNA strands in a test tube was successful when they produced a state of energetic coherence in their hearts through creation of a positive emotional state. Over this seven-week program, you will learn to both uncover the wishes and longings of your heart to tap into your emotions, and learn to increase your heart's coherence through heart rhythm meditation. This combination will greatly enhance the power of your intentions.

The concept of **mindset** is closely related to intention and refers to our beliefs, biases, and attitudes which impact our values and ideals. Where do our intentions and mindset come from? Typically, they are formed by what has been taught and modeled for us by our parents, friends, relatives, and the culture at large.

Often, parenting books are filled with activities and suggestions for behavior management. Unfortunately, the strategies alone rarely solve the problem as they don't address the mindset of the adults involved in the situation. Understanding our mindset helps us clarify or modify our intentions. A successful business coach I know emphasizes the need to know and adjust one's mindset first before applying any strategy to maximize the likelihood of success. This is equally true for parenting and teaching. Anyone who has had an unsuccessful New Year's resolution, despite good intentions and strategies for forward progress, will relate to this! We may think that our intentions and mindset arise from our conscious minds; however, they largely are rooted in our subconscious emotional life and underlying belief system. Often these forces lurking beneath the surface sabotage our efforts. This causes our intention to lose forward momentum and power. By becoming aware of what lies deep in our hearts, we can utilize its power to manifest our intentions. This awareness maximizes the effectiveness of our strategies.

Multiple therapeutic strategies for both children and adults in widespread use today are based on cognitive behavioral therapy. The main idea teaches that emotional reactions and behavioral changes originate with alteration of one's thought patterns. Although this strategy can be useful at times, it ignores the deeper layers of our being. To be more effective with the children in our lives, we need to tap into the heart's wisdom and capitalize on the power of its emotions to connect to deeper, often subconscious, material. By following the method outlined in this book, you will increase your capacity to hear the inner voice of the heart to direct your intentions with power.

Two people can have the intention, "I want to bring out the greatness of my child", yet this will look different in application. For example, a certain level of toughness is valued by parents who know their children are not on an equal playing field with others, so they want to prepare them to be able to withstand injustice. From that perspective, the parent might even be grateful to a bully for providing the opportunity to learn how to deal with them. Another parent might cringe at the idea of preparing a child to be "tough" and might value teaching their child to maintain emotional sensitivity when interacting with the world. I want you to honor your personal intentions and values. Through the activities in this book, you will learn how to unearth intentions which stem from both the depth of your heart and your mind. I hope it is clear that I am leading you on a path which takes into account you and the child's distinctiveness - the antithesis of a cookie-cutter approach.

The heart's voice differs from the voice of the head. I experience my heart's voice as a wish or a longing, and my head's voice speaks more concretely with values and beliefs.

While these levels are connected, "wish" and "longing" are more emotionally charged, and "beliefs" and "values" are more mental. When we hear the words of our heart, it feels different than when the words come from our minds. Our children feel a difference too, depending on where our words come from. They can feel an emotional charge which has the effect of strengthening connection. I will teach you how to move more deeply into your heart so that by Week Seven, your language will have a greater chance of landing in the heart of the child. When the language of greatness lands in the child's heart, real change can occur.

As parents and teachers, we have an advantage in learning to access the power of the heart. We love children! Love is one of the most potent emotions we can use to stimulate the power of the heart. We can lose touch with our underlying love in the chaos of life and in the face of challenging children. Fortunately, it is a short journey back. If you find yourself in the space of emotional disconnection, the fact that you are reading this book demonstrates your intention to improve your current situation. Ruminating on not having the "right feelings" will drain your emotional energy. Turn the energy around and celebrate the greatness of knowing when to seek assistance!

Step one in the Greatness Chair process is to connect with your heart and learn to listen to its voice to uncover your ideals and intentions. This week's activities will help you move into your heart and discover your intentions for the children in your life. Don't worry about getting the right answers or trying to make the list perfect. The list is a starting place and may change as your heart more fully joins the conversation.

For this week, we are not "fixing" or applying strategies with the children yet. I am asking you to make a commitment to yourself to spend at least ten minutes a day listening to your heart. I hope you can see this as an opportunity for sacred space. If you have trouble finding a quiet space as a parent, there is always the bathroom! Be creative and have fun giving yourself time to dream.

WEEK ONE ACTIVITIES

ACTIVITIES FOR YOU

1. Every day, set a timer for ten minutes and find a chair in a quiet space where you can sit up straight with your feet on the ground.

2. Put your hands on your heart.

3. Close your eyes and imagine you can move yourself into your heart. If you are a visual person, you might imagine pulling up a chair and sitting in your heart. When your attention is focused here, your experience will change. You might feel sensations, a heartbeat or pressure in the chest. These are all signals that you are in your heart. If visualization is not your strongest channel, try to just sense your heartbeat under your hands. If you can't feel your physical heart that is okay. It can take time for that to develop. Just put your awareness there with your hands on your chest to help direct your attention to the heart.

4. Now listen. Your mind will chatter away but challenge yourself with the intention, "I want to hear what my heart has to say." You might get flooded with emotion and even tears. If that happens, congratulations! You have touched the emotional heart.

5. When it seems right, add the intention to feel or rekindle love for the children in your life. This may or may not be something you feel instantly. Give yourself the gift of time and patience to practice! What sensations are in your body when you feel love? You might feel a general sense of calmness or a fullness in your chest. If trying to feel love does not bring up a feeling in your heart, switch to a feeling of gratitude for anything in your life and try sensing your body signals again.

6. Start a journal for reflections, insights and "aha" moments. No complete sentences required!

7. While in your heart space, write in your journal, or on the following page, a list of things you would like to see your kids do or qualities you would like to see. Don't overthink this. Record your spontaneous thoughts. Putting your hand on your heart can help you stay focused on the heart's voice. Consider what you love and what you are aiming for.

8. Now repeat steps 5-7 for yourself. Feel compassion for yourself and re-kindle some self-love. Find qualities you would like to nurture in yourself. Think of someone you admire. What qualities do they have that you are attracted to? This is a clue to latent or already-present qualities of greatness in yourself. The qualities we admire in others often reflect our growing edge.

INTENTIONS

Reflect on your values, purpose, meaning, ideals, wishes, and dreams. Use the words which resonate with you. The idea is to get more clarity about your intentions as a parent, as a teacher, or a grandparent and the outcomes you want to see for the children. It could be something like: "I don't want to lose my temper when I get frustrated", "I want the children to listen to me the first time", "I want the children to try harder when they find something difficult", "I want to be more loving", or "I want to help the child see their strengths".

Intentions:

1. _____

2. _____

3. _____

4. _____

5. _____

QUALITIES

What qualities would you like to see in the individual child or children as a group? At this point in the journey we are referring to **your** values and ideals. It is important to be clear about your own biases, as they will affect whether you see something as a problem or not in the child. Eventually we may have to relax some of our perspective of right and wrong to truly support the child but right now, we just want to be aware of our own values and preferences. For instance, consider a child who interrupts and challenges everything the adult says. One parent or teacher may label this as disrespectful and disobedient. Another might value the intense curiosity the child exhibits, seeing it as a sign of intelligence. The first parent might want to develop the quality of patience and the second might want to develop the quality of critical thinking. Try to be honest with yourself so you can uncover your biases. We all have them.

Qualities we want to see develop in the child:

1. _____

2. _____

3. _____

4. _____

5. _____

ACTIVITIES WITH THE KIDS

1. Tell the children you are going to be trying something new over the next few weeks so you can help them discover their greatness. You don't need to explain any further.

2. Have the children put their hands over their hearts and ask them if they can feel their heartbeat.

3. Ask if there is something their heart wants to say. If nothing spontaneous happens, tell them feelings come from the heart and ask if their heart has any feelings. See this as a playful exploration of their heart. You don't need to comment on or judge what they share with you. Simply acknowledge what they say by repeating it back to them, such as, "Oh, your heart says…." Or, "Your heart feels…."

4. You can share with your child what you are discovering in your own heart. This models how to have a dialogue with their heart.

WEEK TWO: ATTENTION

Key concepts: focus, noticing what is going right, discovering what we are devoted to, choice.

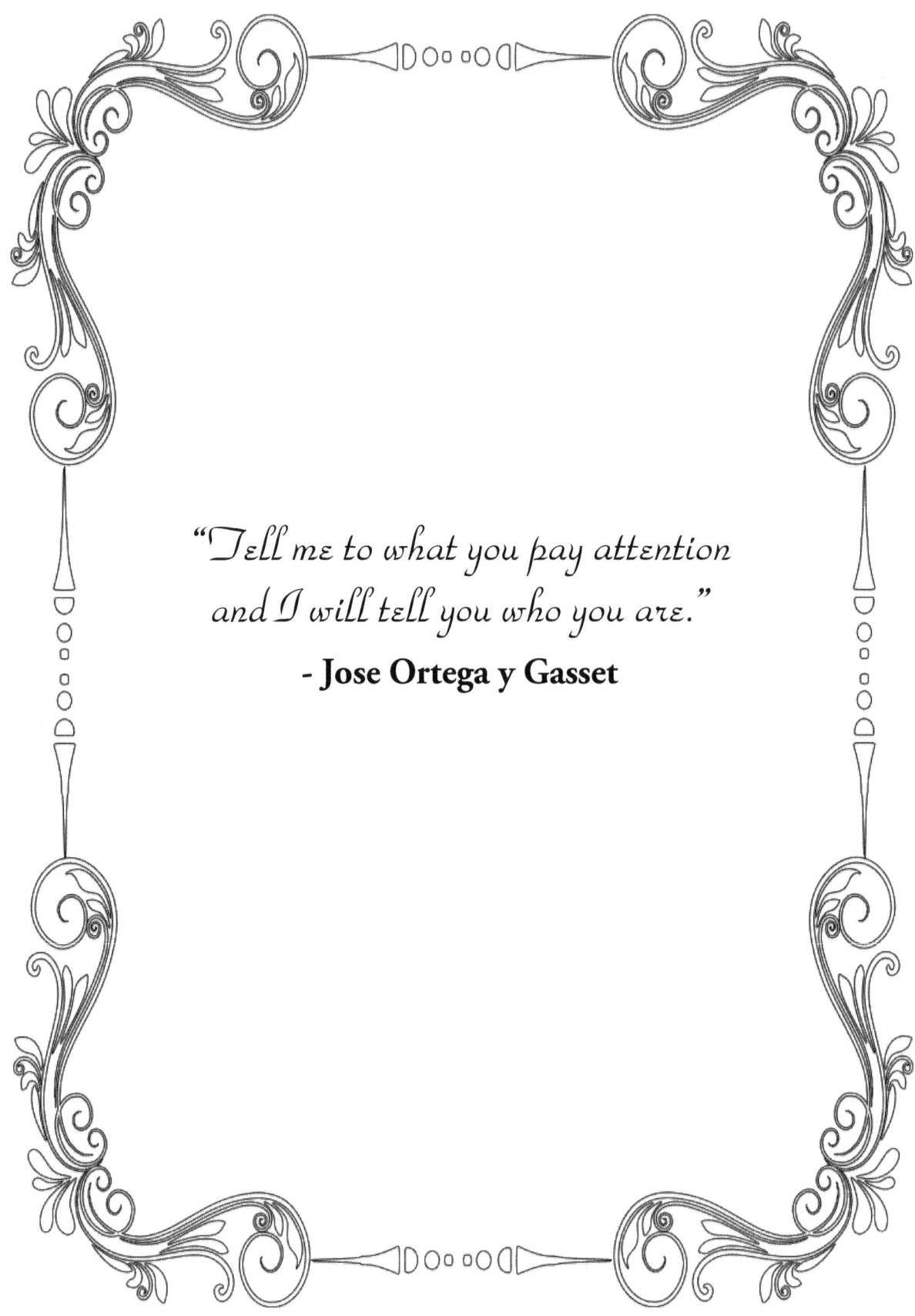

"Tell me to what you pay attention and I will tell you who you are."
- **Jose Ortega y Gasset**

"Pay attention!" Haven't we all heard this incessant refrain, whether it be directed at us or whether we are the speaker of these stinging commands? This is good advice clothed in an ill-fitting garment. It is not specific enough to help children figure out the how or the what. Children are paying attention to something, but it may not be what we have in mind! We are all struggling with focusing our attention these days amidst so many compelling distractions. We and our children are increasingly scattered by short sound bites, rapidly changing visual cues on TV and video, social media posts, and the dings and beeps from our smart phone. We need to practice paying attention with a clear focus and intention.

We are always paying attention to something but it may or may not be where we want to devote our time and energy. This week we will dig deeper into this topic to help us access the power of attention. By considering the related concept of devotion, we will be better equipped to understand ourselves more deeply so we can successfully refocus our attention. Devotion is often thought of as being directed to a person; however, it is a broader concept and not necessarily confined to a personal relationship.

Generally speaking, we are devoted to where we put our time and energy. As parents and teachers, we most likely see ourselves as devoted to children. Understanding what this looks like individually is helpful and moves us into the more profound and meaningful layers of our "why" and "purpose".

> *"He who has a why can endure any how."*
> **- Frederick Nietzsche, 19th century German philosopher.**

Devotion carries an emotional charge and is a heart quality related to love. No one has to tell the lover to pay attention! If we are aware of what our heart wants, it will be easier to focus our mental attention in the proper direction. Some of us are devoted to knowledge, to new insights and innovation, or to truth at all costs. Others are devoted to a cause or to a specific person or group. Others look for the sacred in life whether as seen in ideas, religious rituals or nature. Understanding what we love helps us settle into where we naturally tend to focus our attention. With the addition of this concept of heart-based devotion to our discussion of attention, let us turn to the power of shifting our attention consciously in our dealings with the children and ourselves.

Energy flows where attention is placed. We want to harness energy through where we put our focus and attention. For example, we are upset when our children can't or don't focus their attention when it is needed. This is usually noticed most at school or when we are asking our child to complete a task. We see the outcome of lack of attention - very little gets done!

In physics, energy and work are closely related. Work results from a transfer of energy. So, we want to use this basic principle in our approach. **Focused attention is energy which helps things get done**. It is also the key ingredient as to what gets stronger and what becomes weaker.

The legend of the two wolves from the Cherokee tradition illustrates this well. In the story, a child is aware of a war inside him/herself between good and evil and is distressed over what the outcome will be. A wise elder instructs the child to think of good and evil as two wolves. The wolf they feed will be the stronger one and the winner. This teaches us that our attention is what allows things to grow and prosper. Where we direct our energy is intimately related with the qualities and mindset that we carry with us into the world.

We can use our attention to feed our children in a way that supports their greatness or can inadvertently feed less desirable parts. It is natural to want to pay attention to the child when they are in distress and to uncover what is bothering them. Before children can communicate verbally or non-verbally, we have to do this. When the baby cries we try to figure out where the distress is coming from. Is she hungry, wet, cold? We are detectives in search of the fixable problem. As the child develops and can communicate, we can handle distress in a different way. We don't need to have the same urgency to uncover the feelings or motives behind the behavior. We can focus our attention on what is going right in the moment in order to reset the child back to their greatness. At a later time, we can explore what led to the unwelcome behavior in a moment of calm and self-control for both the child and adult. When a child is showing us their intensity through yelling or hitting, the logical part of the brain is off-line and well-meaning lessons and inquiries into the whys won't register. The child must be back in a state of self-control and calm to collaborate with us in this way.

Too many kids get hooked on the energy of negative attention and they will do everything possible to get it. Love is an energy and children will read all energy as love. This can hook us into power struggles with the children as they seek out negative attention, and the spiral intensifies. Many well-intentioned adults quite innocently get into this spiral by providing loving attention when misbehavior is occurring. Attention equals love to children no matter how they get it!

The essence of conventional parenting is: "I will be alert to and correct my child's faults and applaud their successes so they can thrive at home, at school and eventually, in the wider world." This comes out of a place of responsibility and love. It is well-intentioned and parents feel like they are failing when their efforts don't work. Focusing attention on the "problem" is what I call "upside down energy". I suggest, instead, to turn the energy "right side up", by paying attention to things that are going right instead of going wrong.

Giving our energy to what is going right shifts the equation and draws the child into a relationship which is safe, positive and supportive of their best selves. This can be tricky because we don't want to accidently shower our attention in the midst of problem behavior. We want to wait for any brief moment of reset back to self-regulation before jumping back in with the gift of relationship. For example, a child does not want to share with a sibling and is yelling at or hitting them. We can say, "reset" or "pause". In the brief moment when no misbehavior is happening, we both verbally acknowledge their feelings of frustration and anger simultaneously with the greatness of being willing to fight for what is important to them. We then follow with, "But I see you regained control and are not hitting now in spite of your anger." In this example, the adult is talking about the child's feelings and is mirroring back a quality of greatness. So, we are not ignoring the child's feelings. We are crafting our response to keep the focus on the child's strengths in a moment when the child is not misbehaving or breaking a rule. If we want to make sure we have not misjudged the child's inner state, we can talk with the child later when they are calm to deepen our understanding and make any needed corrections. This empowers the child with their own voice and helps them discover their inner life more fully.

This week, I want you to spend time paying attention to things that are going right instead of what is going wrong. You have to overcome the negativity bias of your brain to do this. We are wired to see problems for survival. Noticing what is going right does not have the same biological imperative as seeing a threat or danger. It takes a lot of focus and attention to shift from the negative to positive. It takes energy to establish a new pattern of reaction. We can rewire our brains to more effortlessly see the positive through the brain's capacity to change, called neuroplasticity. Our brains change by making new and stronger connections depending on where we put our attention.

Intention provides direction and energy for our attention. As discussed in the previous chapter, intention relates to our purpose, meaning, values and what we are devoted to.

This week, relish finding moments of greatness everywhere.

WEEK TWO ACTIVITIES

ACTIVITIES FOR YOU

1. Every day, set a timer for ten minutes and find a chair in a quiet space where you can sit up straight with your feet on the ground .

2. Put your hands on your heart.

3. Close your eyes and imagine you can move yourself into your heart. If you are a visual person, imagine you can pull up a chair and sit in your heart.

4. If visualization is not your strongest channel, see if you can sense your heartbeat under your hands, or pretend you can sense it.

5. Think of a situation that went wrong with your child or student. Keep your hand on your heart! It will help you stay focused there while your mind goes over the incident.

6. While focusing your attention on your heart, try to see what was actually going right in that situation or focus on a quality the child exhibited during the event. For example, if your child was refusing to listen or follow your directions, perhaps the child had the greatness of intense focus on whatever was competing for

his or her attention. Or perhaps the child had great clarity of what was important to him or her. For the sake of this exercise, do not focus on undesirable behaviors. Give yourself permission to let go of the mistakes, misdeeds and rule-breaking.

7. Write about your discoveries or insights in your journal. It can be brief. Put enough to go back someday and remind yourself what your heart had to say.

ACTIVITIES WITH THE KIDS

1. Every day try to notice something going right. Do this when the child is not breaking a rule. For example, perhaps the child is quietly doing their schoolwork or playing with a sibling without arguments. Make a note of what they are doing that is positive. Note this may be an actual behavior like sitting quietly with focus, or the absence of a problematic behavior like not complaining about doing his or her schoolwork. Write it down in this book or your journal.

2. If you feel comfortable, share the observation with the child. You don't need to make a big deal of things or explain yourself. Don't worry about getting the words just right. The child will feel the energy of your intention and attention. You don't need to make a big deal of it or explain yourself. Just deliver the observation about what is going right. If the child rejects it, you can remain quiet or simply verbalize what you noticed or saw. Some children can be very oppositional and start to argue. If this is the case, try to notice something that is hard to refute like, "You are playing quietly right now and not fighting with your sister over toys." Just put your observation out there, bless and release it without any expectation of how it is received, and calmly walk away.

3. Write down the daily observations in your journal or in the book on the next page.

What I noticed going right:

1. _____
2. _____
3. _____
4. _____
5. _____
6. _____
7. _____

WEEK THREE: POSTURE

Key concepts: reset, pause, reflection, stillness, mindset, inner voice

"*Listen to the silence,
it has much to say.*"
- **Rumi**

*It is inner stillness that will
save and transform the world.*"
- **Eckhart Tole**

Posture is more than standing up straight! It involves everything we do with our bodies. We can have a welcoming or a threatening posture. From infancy onward, we learn to read body language and become experts early in life. We all respond to body language largely outside of conscious awareness. Moreover, we are usually unaware of our own posture and how it affects those around us. We will focus on cultivating a posture of both mental and physical stillness . When we learn stillness, we gain easier access to the deeper parts of ourselves, including our heart's wisdom.

For mental stillness, we will use the term "reset" as an invitation to energetically unplug from a stressful situation. In this context, mental stillness doesn't mean that our mind is blank or that we are having no thoughts. Rather, it is a shift of attention to the possibility of greatness by diving into the heart. You will practice resetting in this week's activities.

Think of "reset" as pushing a pause button. This skill will allow us to have more control over where we put our attention and energy. I want to emphasize that the reset ideally is a **brief** pause, the purpose of which is to allow us shift our energetic direction. It does not mean that we "check out" from the situation, but that we briefly allow an interruption to the flow of energetic connection to the child. Depending on the situation, we may need more time to reset ourselves back to a place of stillness. With practice, the resets will get easier and shorter.

The following is a story about a mom who successfully negotiated the problems of her angry, non-engaged teenage daughter with the power of the reset.

> *My 14-year-old daughter was angry and had concerning self-harming behaviors. When I tried to give her positive recognition for things that were going right instead of commenting on the problems, my daughter did not believe me and thought my words were inauthentic.*

Despite the mother's many attempts to speak from her heart, her daughter would not let her words in. Mom switched course and focused instead on her own energetic shift. When her daughter was provocative, she reset herself internally to a calm place to just "be" with her quietly without an energetic connection. Mom wasn't giving a lecture or expressing emotion. Her daughter quieted and noted the shift. Once her daughter was quiet, Mom "turned back on" and gave a simple recognition like "I'm glad you shared that with me" to signal the reconnection. She discovered that her power was in her internal energy shift and that she could control the flow of energy between them. Over time, Mom was able to use the kind of greatness recognitions that form the backbone of this book, but first she had to manage her own energy for them to work effectively.

"By adopting a certain physical posture, a resonant chord is struck in spirit."

– Bruce Lee

To tap into the power of **physical** posture, we will practice a period of physical quietude called the monolithic posture. This is the royal posture seen in several statues which remain from ancient Egypt, such as The Colossal Group of Amenhotep III and Queen Tiy (Cairo Museum) depicted in the picture at the beginning of this chapter. The serenity on their faces signals the peaceful and joyful state of stillness. A still body helps us slow down so we can take a pause, reset and focus inward to hear our heart's voice. Think of a pool of water with turbulence on the surface. This is our beautiful mind at work. We want to develop the ability to calm the waters of our usual, conscious mental chatter and judgments in order to open up to the wider perspective offered by the intelligence of our heart. Then, by pulling our mind back into the picture with our heart, we have a potent combination. Our heart sets the intention, our mind directs the attention, and we are able to move in the direction of becoming a mirror to reflect back the unique greatness of the children. It is imperative to polish the mirror of our heart in order to reflect the child's truth back to them. While this may sound abstract, following each week's exercises will help you master this ability.

A still body will also stop us from signaling unwanted emotions when in conflict with our children. Children read our body language and pick up on feelings that we think we are hiding by not verbalizing them. They react to these unconscious messages we convey with our bodies. Children will respond to non-verbal communication before hearing our words. Facial expression and tone of voice are two particularly strong non-verbal signals. Muscle tension and posture, or how we hold ourselves in other areas of the body, convey powerful information as well. We are generally unaware of the non-verbal signals we are giving off and may even deny them when confronted. For instance, perhaps someone has asked you to "stop yelling" and you are positive you did not have a raised voice!

Our mindset can also be a "mental" posture towards someone or something. One critical mental posture to become familiar with is that of being reflective. When we want to accomplish something, physical movement is usually involved. Reflectiveness is a slowing down and waiting without urgency or expectation. This week make the intention to start each day reflectively even if it is only a brief minute or so. If there are inspirational words that move you, recite or read them. Perhaps place a book of quotes or poems on your bed stand and reach for it first thing to set the tone for your day.

Enter your day slowly with an intention of reflection instead of task orientation.

ACTIVITIES FOR YOU

1. Every day, set a timer for ten minutes and find a chair in a quiet space where you can sit up straight with your feet on the ground.

2. Put your hands on your heart.

3. Commit to holding your body still. If your back is uncomfortable, place some pillows behind you with the aim of being upright with a straight spine. If this is not possible for you due to physical limitations, another option is standing up or lying down. Sitting upright is preferred as it allows our spine to work like an energetic antenna conducting our energy more efficiently.

4. Become aware of your breath.

5. Practice resets by taking a few breaths into your heart. The mind will quiet with both a still body and focused attention on breath and heart. Don't concern yourself with the depth of the breath this week but allow it to slow and deepen if it happens naturally. Experiment with a feeling of love or gratitude as you breathe and see if that strengthens your feelings of well-being.

6. Practice resets during the day. You can do this anytime. It is easiest to practice when things are calm or there is only a mild irritant. Eventually you will be able to do this when the stakes are high and you are on the verge of negative reactivity to a challenging situation. The reset is simply putting your awareness on your breath and heart. If it helps, put your hand on your heart or wrap your arms around your chest like you are holding the heart area. Closing your eyes may help your visualization of the breath going into your heart. If closing your eyes is stressful, keep them open. Adding a feeling of love or gratitude while breathing into your heart can enhance feelings of peace and well-being. Practicing the reset will also increase your heart's coherence and power to set the right atmosphere for the eventual use of the Greatness Chair.

ACTIVITIES WITH THE KIDS

1. Practice seeing and noticing in the moment without judgement.

2. Watch your child (or anyone for that matter) and, in your mind or on paper, note what you see. Write observable facts, not your interpretation of what you are looking at. It could be simply, "Anne has a blue shirt and white pants on. She is leaning over and touching her blocks. She is not talking and her eyes are fixed on the tower she is building."

3. If there is a question of safety for the child or others, intervene to keep everyone safe. Act from a position of stillness and reset with minimum energy. Do what is necessary without drama, explanations, lecturing or verbal corrections.

4. Play "red light/green light" with your kids if it is age appropriate. This is the perfect game to help children shift from movement to stillness and reset. A variation on this game which can work for all ages is to add a shift in awareness to breath and heart by asking the children to put their hands on their heart and feel their breath enter and leave from that place during the red light. For older kids, make this fun. Put on music and have them dance for the green light.

WEEK FOUR: SENSATION

Key concepts: interoception, neuroception, polyvagal theory, fight, flight and freeze, the five senses, proprioception, heartbeat, sensing the heart field.

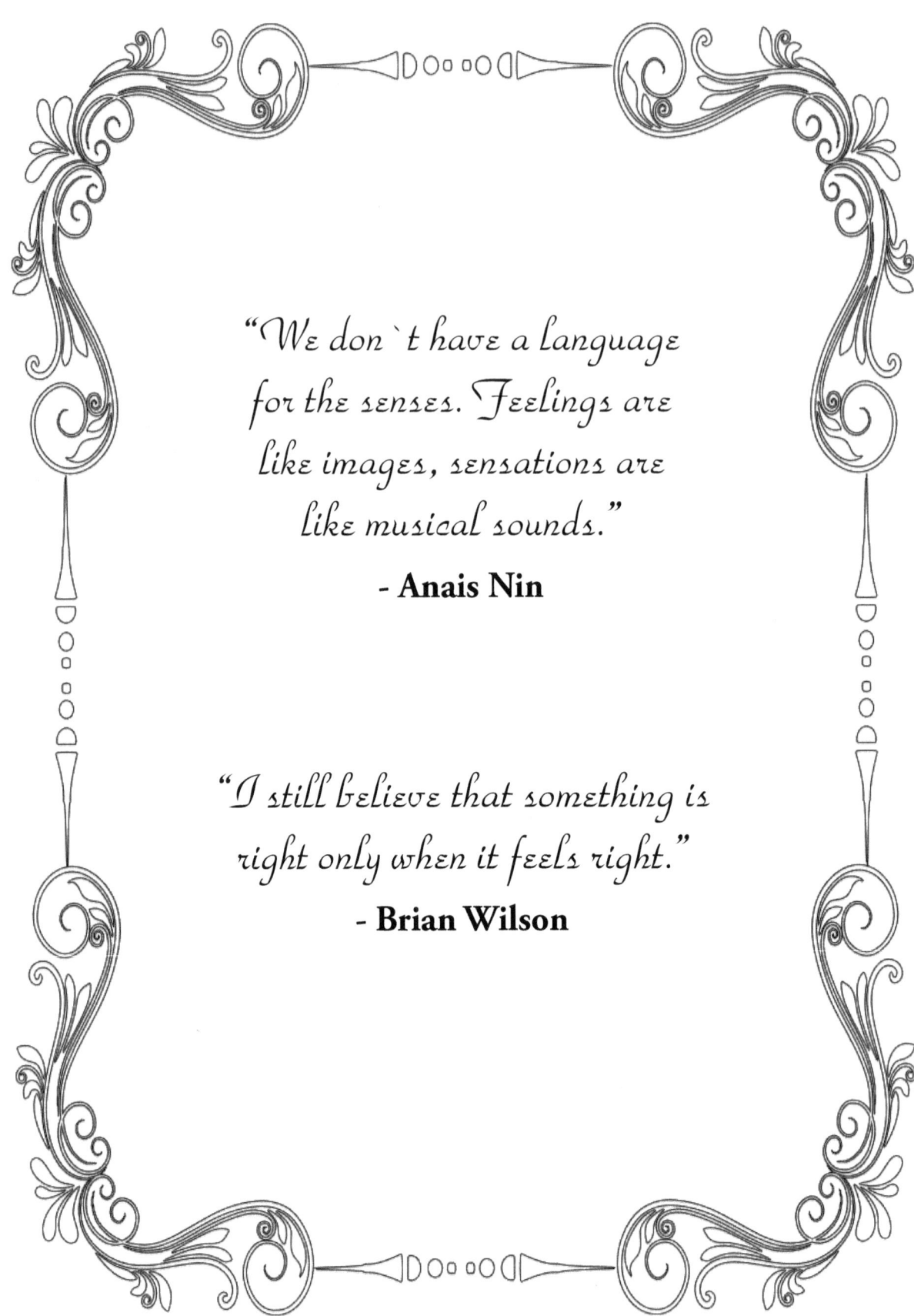

"We don`t have a language for the senses. Feelings are like images, sensations are like musical sounds."
- **Anais Nin**

"I still believe that something is right only when it feels right."
- **Brian Wilson**

Sensation refers to receiving input from both the inner and outer world. External sensory information comes into us through the six senses – vision, touch, smell, taste, hearing and proprioception. Proprioception is our sense of movement and position in space. This is the sense that tells us, for example, that our hand is raised, or whether we are smiling or frowning.

We have other senses that allow us to experience the world from the inside, called interoception. This inner sensory system related to bodily cues allows us to have the experience of embodiment. Examples include sensing thirst, hunger, our heartbeat, the need to urinate, pain or depth of breath.

Feeling sensations in our bodies also gives us clues about our emotional state. Are we relaxed? Tense? Do we have pain in our body? Stiffness? Researchers have mapped where emotions are felt in the body with consistent results cross-culturally. Happiness and love spark the most widespread activity in the body, with very high levels of sensation in the heart and head. Depression had the opposite effect, with very little or no sensation reported in the body. Fear and anxiety triggered strong sensations mainly in the chest. Anger showed increased sensations in the head , chest and arms.

There are many things to observe within our bodies and we generally do not pay attention to its signals until things are extreme. Our body clues also tell us where we fall on the spectrum of stress. Are we in a fight-or-flight state? Are we in a freeze or dissociated state? Are we at ease and relaxed? We can also sense if we are ready for social connection or not. When interacting with children, we want to be able to recognize if we are in the optimal state for connection and, if not, know how to find our way back quickly. If you follow the exercises in this book each week, you will improve this ability to return to your own "window of tolerance" by resetting your nervous system back to an optimal state for connection.

We believe our senses are feeding us factual information about the world, but that is not necessarily true. Everything is filtered through our personal physiology and nervous system. Even colors look different between individuals. Our bodies may be warning us that we are under threat when no danger is present. That is the basis of the trauma response - our nervous system perceives a threat based on previous experiences and thinks the trauma is happening again in the present.

Children and adults with severe, prolonged or early exposure to adverse experiences are particularly vulnerable to misreading incoming external or internal sensory input due to shifts in the way sensory information is handled by the traumatized brain. Sensory cues are more easily misinterpreted as signals of danger, and thus trigger inappropriate stress responses. This can manifest as agitation or shut-down. An extreme reaction can cause disconnection from the body, called dissociation.

"The senses are a kind of reason. Taste, touch and smell, hearing and seeing, are not merely means to sensation, enjoyable or otherwise, but they are also a means to knowledge."

- Joseph Campbell

Why is reading our bodily cues important for bringing out greatness in children and ourselves? We need to develop the ability to read our inner bodily cues so we understand what state we are in. We also need to experience these inner states and sensations without being triggered into a stress response. When we can do this, we are in the optimal state for social connection with ourselves and others. It is from this place of ease and safety that we can experience our best selves and see it in others. **We and our children need to feel safe internally to move into greatness.** When the body does not feel safe, we cannot direct our attention to the positive since we are in survival mode. It can be difficult to learn to step into bodily safety but **we can learn to use the sensations of heartbeat and breath through the practice of heart rhythm meditation to bring the needed reset to the body to allow us to move into the energy of greatness.**

A popular way to conceptualize these different emotional states of stress and safety was developed by Leah Kuypers in 2011 and is referred to as the "Zones of Regulation". Widely implemented in school SEL (Social Emotional Learning) programs, it outlines four possible emotional zones - red, blue, yellow and green. Depending on which state the child is in, he or she had greater or lesser arousal levels and emotional control. Generally speaking, the green zone is happy, calm, and focused; the red zone is anger or out of control; the blue zone is low arousal from sadness, fatigue, boredom or illness; and the yellow pathway is excited, silly, hyper or nervous. The child is considered optimally ready to learn when in the green zone.

Recent work in the understanding of stress and how trauma affects the nervous system has relied heavily on the polyvagal theory developed by Stephen Porges, Ph.D. It has helped us understand how our mammalian nervous system functions optimally for social connection. In this book, we will work with a three-zone model of regulation rather than four outlined by Kuypers to align it more clearly with the polyvagal theory. This model will remove the yellow zone and integrate those behaviors partly into the red zone and partly into the green zone. The yellow zone is confusing because it includes high arousal states that are both positive (e.g. silliness, excitement) and negative (e.g. hyperactivity and nervousness). A child in the high arousal yellow zone may or may not be in a state compatible with focus and social connection. By removing the yellow zone from our framework, it is easier to identify if the child is ready for connection.

For our purposes, we will call the red pathway "fight or flight", the blue pathway "dissociation and disengagement", and the green pathway "safety and ease" (where social engagement can occur). In polyvagal theory, the red zone is correlated with sympathetic nervous system dominance, the blue zone is dorsal vagal dominance, and the green zone is ventral vagal dominance. I include these neurophysiologic details for those familiar with polyvagal theory, but understanding these concepts is not important to successfully complete the steps of this book. What is important is understanding how to recognize these states in ourselves by reading our internal body cues, and how to recognize these states in others using their external cues.

Children's actions and behaviors depend on which pathway their nervous system is in. The same is true for us. We must be in the green zone to lead children there. This is referred to as co-regulation and it is the adult's job to orchestrate this. Just like a conductor who signals the rhythm with his or her arms to the musicians, we must set the rhythm for the children. All health depends on rhythm, and it is important to become masters of setting the proper rhythm at the right time.

Before we can do this, we must be able to sense whether we are in the green zone or not. If we are not in the green zone, it is can be a signal that a reset is needed.

> *"Sensations of peace, joy and love will enter into you. They will be very subtle at first. Then they will grow stronger."*
>
> **- Frederick Lenz**

The most powerful way for us to reset to the rhythm of social connection and safety is to use practices which acknowledge the fact that the heart is the largest generator of energy in the body. The strength and shape of the energy field we can create with our heart is affected by our breathing pattern. When our breath changes, our emotions and the energetic heart field changes. It is the energetic heart field that sets both bodily rhythms and the emotional atmosphere for the child to bathe in. In week five, you will learn how to coordinate your breath with your heartbeat to maximize these effects. This week we will start by learning to sense these two rhythms in our body without trying to change them.

I will ask you to start sensing for yourself and the child which of these three zones you are in. It is not always easy to determine this. We may feel relaxed and assume we are in the green zone, but physiologic measurements of pulse, heart rate, or blood pressure might tell another story. The extremes of each state are easiest to identify and it takes practice to read subtler clues.

Here is a list of possible physical manifestations of each state in children as adapted from the book, *Beyond Behaviors* by Monica Delahooke (2019).

ZONES OF REGULATION CHART

BLUE: Shutting Down		
Blank face	Mouth turned down	Sad
Voice is flat or too soft	Slow movements or child seems "frozen"	Slumped/slouching
Disinterested	Wanders aimlessly	Makes few sounds
Looks at things more than people	Looks tired	Looks away or down for a long time
Glazed/glassy eyes, "deer in headlights" look	Slow to start moving	

RED: Fight or Flight		
Eyes darting around room	Eyes squinted or closed	Direct, intense eye contact
Constant motion	Biting, kicking, jumping, throwing	Threatening gestures
High pitched yelling, crying or screaming	Arched back, tense body position	Hostile or grumpy voice
Sarcastic	Frown, grimace or fake, forced smile	Anger or disgust on face
Fast or impulsive movements	Clenched jaw, teeth	

GREEN: Social		
Bright, shiny eyes	Alert, taking in information	Looks directly at people
Body relaxed	Balanced and coordinated movements	Smiling
Can express all emotions	Laughing	Vocal tone modulates and is expressive
Child will hug or mold to the adult if touched	Movements change naturally in response to the environment	Shows joy
Neutral expression	Looks away for breaks but then resumes eye contact	

Although there is overlap in the above table between children and adults, I want to add more possibilities for us to tune into our adult states.

1. Would you be annoyed if interrupted right now from whatever you are doing? This could be a task or an interruption while you are speaking. If the answer is yes, you were in or switched quickly into the red zone.

2. Have you felt impatient listening to another person speak? Have you already thought about what you want to say and tuned them out? This is also the red zone.

3. If you have found yourself waiting in a line and been irritated that the line is moving too slow, this is a red zone state.

4. Have you ever been happily absorbed in a project unless you were interrupted? For example, if someone interrupted me while typing these words, I would be mildly annoyed as I am in the red zone of focused concentration (a high arousal state). The red zone does not always look like fight-or-flight unless pushed there by external circumstances. Likewise, imagine a child who is focused on their video game or tablet. I bet you can guess what the reaction is if you suddenly interrupt them!

5. Have you suddenly gone blank and lost your train of thought during a conversation? This is the blue zone.

6. Have you ever taken a walk and found yourself scanning the scenery with wonder and curiosity instead of running through your "to do" list? This is the green zone.

ACTIVITIES FOR YOU

1. Every day, set a timer for ten minutes and find a chair in a quiet space where you can sit up straight with your feet on the ground .

2. Put your hands on your heart.

3. Commit to holding your body still. If your back is uncomfortable, place some pillows behind you with the aim of being upright with a straight spine.

4. Become aware of your breath and try to feel your heartbeat or pulse somewhere in your body. The sensation of the heartbeat and breath is constantly communicating information to you. Notice if you are breathing through your mouth or nose. Is your inhale or exhale longer? Try to observe without intentionally changing anything. For many of us, just putting our attention on our breath changes it and it gets deeper. Don't stop that if it happens but keep paying attention to what your breath does naturally.

5. Play a piece of music which moves you, and try to sense your heart from the inside. Can you feel sensations in your chest? You might feel things such as expansion, pain, pressure or heat. These are physical manifestations of your heart field.

6. In your journal, write down these observations. Most likely, your breath and heartbeat will be different on different days. That is normal.

7. Set a timer on your watch or phone for a few times during the day. Then turn inward and see if you can identify whether you are - in the green, red or blue zone? A clue might be asking yourself, "If someone approached me right now, how would I react?" Would I want to withdraw or connect?

8. Pick a few times during the day and see if you can figure out where your child is on the green, blue or red spectrum. Is there any connection or correlation to your state?

9. During a difficult interaction with the child, observe which zone you are both in. Is there a connection?

Pick three times during the day and notice if YOU are in the green, blue or red zone. Write the color in the box. Refer back to the Zone of Regulation chart for reference.

	Time #1	Time #2	Time #3
Monday			
Tuesday			
Wednesday			
Thursday			
Friday			
Saturday			
Sunday			
Totals	R__ B__ G__	R__ B__ G__	R__ B__ G__

Pick three times during the day and notice if your CHILD is in the green, blue or red zone. Write the color in the box. Refer back to the Zone of Regulation chart for reference.

	Time #1	Time #2	Time #3
Monday			
Tuesday			
Wednesday			
Thursday			
Friday			
Saturday			
Sunday			
Totals	R__ B__ G__	R__ B__ G__	R__ B__ G__

ACTIVITIES WITH THE KIDS

1. Explore the inner senses. Pick several objects which can be held and explored by the child but don't let them see the object ahead of time. Try to find objects that have different textures and shapes. Ask your child to close their eyes and explore the object through any of their senses except sight. Ask them to describe what they experience. They may or may not have words to describe what they feel. If they need prompting you can ask about shape, texture, temperature, smell or taste. You can alternate objects and ask how they are different or the same. That might generate more observations. Tell the child there is no right answer. The goal of this exercise is to have children become more aware of their non-visual senses and tune into the variety of sensory information from the inside.

2. Explore the outer senses - smell, taste, hearing, sight, touch, temperature, and proprioception with open eyes. Proprioception is how something feels in space.

Have the child just slow down and tune into the experience. Meal time is a good opportunity to experience all of these. For proprioception, have them slowly raise the eating utensil to their mouth and tune into how the hand and arm feel at different points in space.

3. When your child is calm, ask them if they can feel anything inside their bodies. If they are not sure, ask if they feel anything in their belly, their chest, their hands, or their face. Can they describe the feeling? This is not easy for many people, and they may need many attempts. I suggest you try it daily to help the child tune into their insides.

4. After the child has practiced trying to sense the body during periods of calm, ask them the same question during an intense positive or negative feeling. What do you feel in your body? If they are not sure, ask if they feel anything in their belly, their chest, their hands, or their face. Can they describe the feeling? Don't comment on their answer, just acknowledge it. If they can't feel anything, explain how emotions feel in your body, such as happiness or anger as it may help them focus their attention on certain possibilities.

5. See if you can discover any sensory activities that calm or delight your child. Not all children respond to sensory input or touch in the same way. Become sensitive to whether you are taking the child out of their comfort zone. For example, a tickling game might be fun or it might feel overwhelming. A hug might be perfect at one time but feel intrusive at another time. Wrapping up in a blanket might be soothing. Taking a bath might be relaxing.

6. Have your child put their hand on their chest and ask if they can feel their heartbeat. If not, have them jump up and down a few times and repeat the exercise. Do this with them to help you become more aware of your own heartbeat.

WEEK FIVE: INSPIRATION

Key concepts: full breath, inhalation, exhalation, consciousness, new perspectives, creativity, rhythm, coherence

"There is one way of breathing
that is shameful and constricted.
Then there's another way: a breath
of love that takes you all the way to infinity."
- **Rumi**

"As long as you are breathing,
it's never too late to
start a new beginning."
– **Anonymous**

We generally associate inspiration with new ideas, the ability to see things from a wider or novel perspective, our intuition, our muse, or our inner guidance. We all have the capacity for inspiration, but it can always be strengthened. Every child and situation brings new demands for our ingenuity, as children are not made with a cookie cutter.

> *"Change your breathing, change your life."*
> **- Anonymous**

Inspiration also refers to inhalation of breath. This week we will tap into the power of breath to inspire our minds. Conscious, full, rhythmic breath coupled with the heartbeat is the master switch to unleashing greater creativity and inspiration when dealing with the children in our lives. This week you will learn full, rhythmic, conscious breath. By coupling breath with heartbeat, we will be experiencing heart rhythm meditation. While this will probably take more than a week to master, it is a potent way to unleash our inner power to guide the children close to us more effectively.

We typically do not pay attention to our breathing unless we are out of breath or feel like we need more air, but our inhalation and exhalation patterns have a huge effect on our state of mind. How we breathe (through our nose or our mouth), how quickly we breathe, and the quality of our breathing (the rhythm and depth) are important variables that we can use to steady ourselves.

> *"Deep breaths are like little love notes to your body."*
> **- Anonymous**

Breath is the medium between the inner life and the outer life. When we use the breath consciously, we balance the rhythms in our body and strengthen the heart field.

A deep, full breath intensifies the energy field of our heart. Think of breath as recharging the heart battery. When our heart is full of energy, we will be inspired and our sense of joy and optimism will be enhanced with whatever we are doing.

> *"When you own your own breath, nobody can steal your peace."*
>
> **- Anonymous**

As the adult in the room, we the have power to set the tone and atmosphere by how we use our breath. One of my meditation teachers likes to say, "The person with the most breath in the room wins." This does not mean the person using the most breath yells or speaks more loudly! It means the individual who can use their breath to optimize their heart energy field will both set the tone and be the most influential person in any gathering.

Under normal conditions of unconscious respiration, our breath changes as our emotions change. Holding the breath when fearful or rapid breathing when angered are two common examples. When we pay attention to our breath, we can turn this relationship around and have the ability to change our emotions through how we breathe. Conscious breathing also sets in motion a change which facilitates the release of unconscious material, which may appear in the form of new ideas, memories or pictures. This is a frequent occurrence and may be related to the fact that conscious breathing frees up the lower parts of our brain that normally regulate respiration. A conscious breathing practice can stimulate more emotion while also providing an opportunity to experience and integrate the emotions under conditions that the brain perceives as safe. While this process is unfolding, we want to be mindful of not losing track of our breath or our heartbeat to anchor us in the experience.

Inhalations and exhalations typically are not equal. You will discover this week whether you tend to inhale or exhale for a longer time. Generally speaking, those who have a longer exhale tend to be doers and may have trouble letting other people or new ideas in. Those with long inhales compared to exhales may take in a lot of information from their environment but have difficulty translating their ideas into action. We need to receive the energy of breath to keep the spark of inspiration going as parents and teachers.

When our heart is full of energy, we can act on our inspirations vigorously, with less chance of burnout. Burnout is a lack of energy. We need to stoke the fire of our heart again with breath.

Enjoy the gift of breath and heartbeat to inspire your next level of greatness.

ACTIVITIES FOR YOU

1. Every day, set a timer for ten minutes and find a chair in a quiet space where you can sit up straight with your feet on the ground .

2. Put your hands on your heart.

3. Commit to holding your body still. If your back is uncomfortable, place some pillows behind you with the aim of being upright with a straight spine.

4. Become aware of your breath and try to feel your heartbeat or pulse somewhere in your body. The sensation of the heartbeat and breath is constantly communicating information to you. Notice if you are breathing through your mouth or nose. Is your inhale or exhale longer?

5. Intentionally deepen your breath and make the inhale and exhale even. At the end of your exhale, squeeze your abdomen back to your spine to get all the air out. This will allow for a deeper inhale. At the top of the inhale see if you can go a little further. At the beginning, a count of six or eight is typical for the inhale and exhale. You may have to adjust the length of the breath to match the exhale and inhale for a rhythmic breath. For example, if you can only inhale to a count of six, then match the exhale to the same count. Eventually things will even out. I recommend aiming for a count of eight in and eight out with no stopping after the inhale or exhale.

6. Now try to sense your pulse or heartbeat in your chest. If you can feel it easily, use the heartbeat as the counter for your breath length. Ideally, allow for eight heartbeats on the inhale and eight on the exhale. If you can't feel your heartbeat, try putting your hand on your heart and, using your other hand, wrap it around your wrist just below the thumb and see if you can feel the pulse. Another alter-

native is to hold your breath after the inhale and try sensing your heartbeat on the hold. If you find your heartbeat while holding your breath, resume rhythmic breathing and try to sense it without a hold. It is common to not be able to feel the heartbeat consistently throughout the entire breathing cycle at first. Continue the count based on what you think your heart rhythm is even if you can't clearly feel it. During this conscious breathing exercise, your mind is likely to get quite active with memories, ideas, feelings, colors or pictures. Let them in, but simultaneously keep your attention on the coordination of breath and heartbeats.

7. At a minimum, do a full, rhythmic conscious breath for ten minutes even if you can't feel your heartbeat. If you practice, it will likely appear.

8. Periodically during the day, notice your breath. Are you holding your breath? Are you breathing through your mouth or your nose? Now take a few deep breaths in and out your nose with an awareness of your heart and notice any changes. Do your thoughts change? Do your emotions change? Your breath has the power to shift your consciousness and emotions.

ACTIVITIES WITH THE KIDS

1. Practice breathing activities with the children. It is not necessary to emphasize a full, rhythmic deep breath or counting heartbeats at this stage. We just want the children to become aware of their breath and their hearts.

2. For the exhale, try a cue like, "Blow out the candles." For the inhale, try a cue like, "Smell the roses," or "Sip in air through a straw." Use your imagination to create cues which are meaningful to the children in your life.

3. Have the child exhale on their hand and feel their breath. This makes it more concrete.

4. Have the child put their hand on their heart while breathing and direct them to slow their breath down. You can count for them.

5. Another method for the exhale is to have them hum on the outbreath. This is very relaxing to the nervous system. Use your imagination here. For example, you can direct the child to listen to the sound, or feel it in their chest.

6. Direct the child to take a breath into their heart during a moment of stress. If you practice the technique while the child is calm, they will have better success using it during periods of stress or dysregulation.

WEEK SIX: INVOCATION

Key concepts: soul qualities, emotionally rich and positive vocabulary, mirroring greatness in the moment

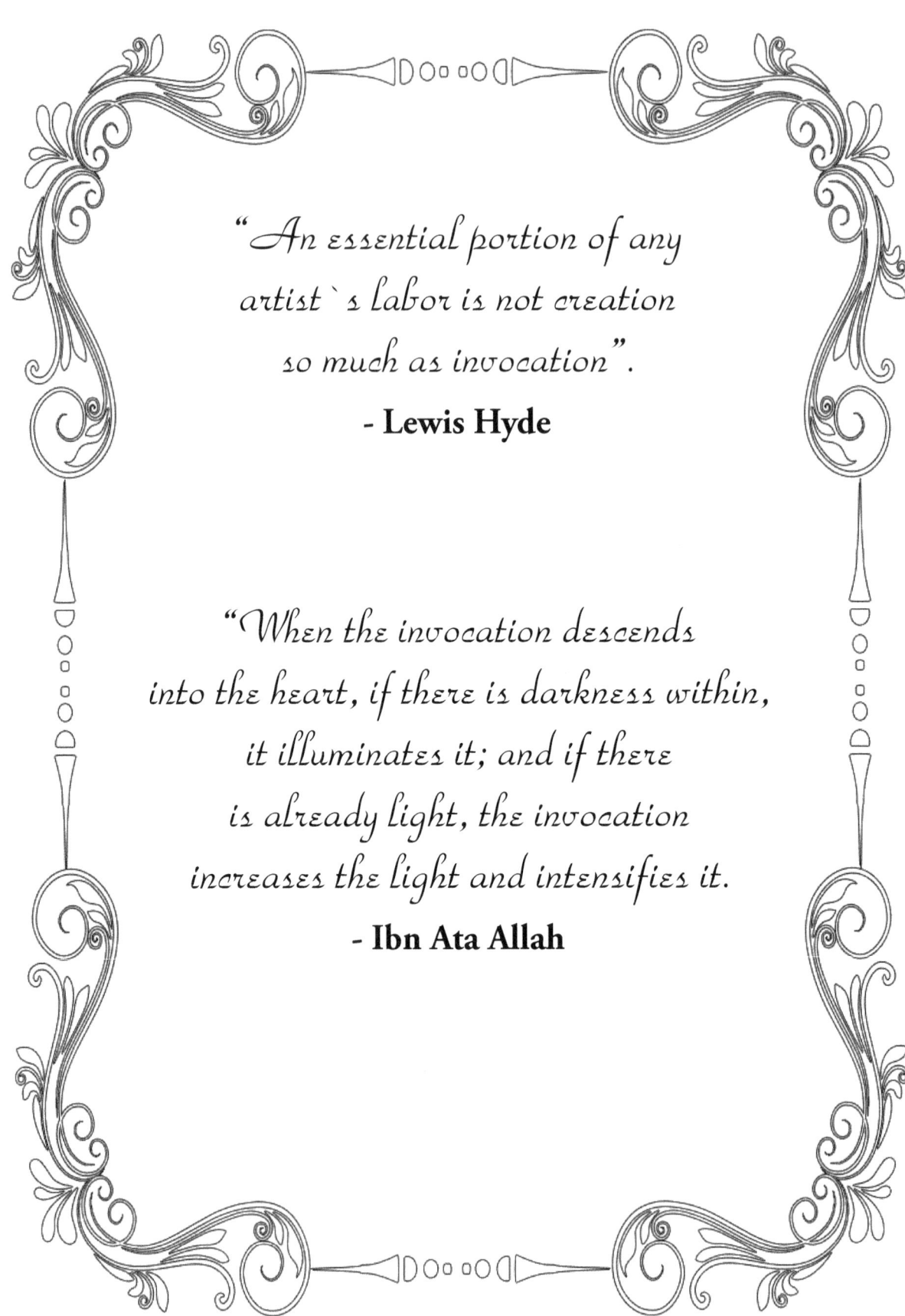

"An essential portion of any artist`s labor is not creation so much as invocation".
- **Lewis Hyde**

"When the invocation descends into the heart, if there is darkness within, it illuminates it; and if there is already light, the invocation increases the light and intensifies it.
- **Ibn Ata Allah**

Invocation means calling forth what we want to see in our children and students. Which qualities or behaviors are important to us? This requires clarification of our values and expectations and challenges us to grow our emotional vocabulary in order to describe what we notice. In Week One we spent some time clarifying the qualities we want to see in our children. Now we are going a step further to integrate this with how these qualities are currently showing up in the child's actions or behaviors.

Many of us are aware that children tend to rise to the expectations of the teacher or parent. I am reminded of a recent story told by a journalist about his earlier life as a troubled teen. He made it clear that while he was a teenager, he had been all too happy to comply with the labels applied to him. Unfortunately, the labels reflected the worst in him.

The most common methods used for implementation of our expectations are: non-specific words of praise like "good job", material rewards, or the absence of yelling or punishment. At school, an additional method of implementation is that of grading and test scores.

Most commonly, a child's success with self-regulation and exhibiting positive qualities goes unnoticed. It fades into the background because we tend to focus our attention on problems that need solving. This is a natural evolutionary tendency of our brain in order to help us survive. Shifting this hard-wired negativity bias of the brain requires effort and specific actions for retraining so we can improve our ability to focus on what is going right.

A powerful way to implement our expectations is through invocation. Invocation is using words which highlight the greatness present in the moment. We want to not only strengthen the greatness which is obvious in the child, but amplify any sliver of greatness still under development. A common example would be how we praise any effort a child makes in the direction of walking before they perfect that skill. We do this naturally when a child is very young, but tend to stop doing this as the child ages and forget that every new skill requires baby steps. We need to see and mirror the developing potential in children because they are still learning about themselves and their unique gifts. Having someone who can mirror aspects of greatness to the child is extremely powerful and will have a strong effect on the child's developing self-concept. Children internalize their self-concept by what others say or do to them. We can fill them with their failures and deficiencies, or we can shine the light on what is already perfect. Although this sounds contradictory, I want you to consider that everything is perfect as it is but can always be improved. If we take this stance, it will help guide our attention to finding moments of greatness.

Everything I have written above about the children needing a mirror is true for ourselves as well. It may be difficult to identify our own greatness or our potentials clearly. We may tend to reflect back our inadequacies. It is a rare gift as an adult to have someone who both sees the best in us and can verbalize it. Often, we hear praise for meeting the expectations of others. This is different than being seen for our own unique greatness qualities. For instance, our boss notices that we show up to work every day on time. That would be a welcome acknowledgment for most of us but it reflects the needs and interests of our employer. If, however, our employer commented on how our punctuality showed our sense of dedication or responsibility, that would point to qualities in ourselves or ideals we hold. This is much more powerful mirroring. It tells us who we are on a deeper level. That kind of observation connects us to our internalized ideals and values. We feel seen.

By practicing heart rhythm meditation as taught in previous weeks, we are polishing the mirror of our heart and retraining our nervous system toward the regulation needed to provide a container of safety for us and the child. This helps us start to notice things about children through the softer, kinder eyes of the heart and reflect back what we see with less harsh judgements. As we step into our best selves, we will bring the children with us and move into ever-expanding levels of greatness.

Once we have an open heart, we still need to find words to communicate our observations of greatness in an emotionally nutritious manner so it lands in the heart of the child. For most of us, our vocabulary for positivity is tiny compared to that for negativity. We need to make a conscious effort to expand our vocabulary of greatness. Consider a child who is playing quietly, building Legos with their sibling. What qualities are they showing? Some examples might be: focus, teamwork, cooperation, creativity, exploring new ideas, sharing, perseverance, enjoyment, respect, relaxation, friendliness, curiosity, composure, accuracy, or attentiveness.

We can also translate the emotions we observe into greatness qualities. For example, anger is strength and energy, fear involves the wisdom of protection and preservation, guilt shows our values and ideals, and so on.

Our words are sacred utterances which reach deeply into the soul of the child. Everything, including your tone of voice, your physical gestures and the emotional atmosphere you create will change if you believe in the sacredness of your words. **The language of greatness combines the language of love with the eagle eyes of the heart to see the divine being in front of us.**

Invocation is a method to implement our intentions through the use of our words. The challenge is to notice both the greatness qualities already present in the child while simultaneously leading them along a path of good character in line with our values. Although there are values which tend to have agreement cross-culturally, good character means different things to different people and comes from a variety of influences which may include personal history, religious background or socio-cultural factors. In our eagerness to instill "good character" we can overlook the progress the child may already be exhibiting in those areas. There is a delicate balancing act between accepting the truth of the moment and seeing where the child can improve. By strongly energizing the child with our invocations for the greatness already present, the child will have greater inner strength to navigate across the rough waters of development on the way to maturity.

It is important to remember that, in order to accept where the child is on their journey, we need to be able to assess ourselves with the same level of compassion and acceptance. This is not easy for many of us, especially for us raised by well-intentioned adults whose high standards came across in a way that left shame in its wake. Bringing out the best in children is a parallel process between them and us. My wish is for you to embrace this without feelings of guilt or shame as there is a natural tendency in all of us for growth and regeneration if we allow the process to move forward.

ACTIVITIES FOR YOU

1. Commit to ten minutes of heart rhythm meditation every day.

   a. Sit up straight in a chair with your feet on the ground.

   b. Commit to holding your body still. If your back is uncomfortable, place some pillows behind you with the aim of being upright with a straight spine.

   c. Become aware of your breath for a few cycles and just notice how the inhale and exhale are for you today without an intervention.

   d. Intentionally deepen your breath and make the inhale and exhale even. At the end of your exhale, squeeze your abdomen back to your spine to get all the air out. This will allow for a deeper inhale. At the top of the inhale see if you can go a little further. At the beginning, a count of six or eight is typical for the inhale and exhale. You may have to adjust the length of the breath to match the exhale and inhale for a rhythmic breath. For example, if you can only inhale to a count of six, then match the exhale to the same count. Eventually things will even out. I recommend aiming for a count of eight in and eight out with no stopping after the inhale or exhale.

   e. Now try to sense your pulse or heartbeat. If you can feel it easily, use the heartbeat as the counter for your breath length. If you can't feel it, try putting your hand on your heart, and using your other hand, wrap it around your wrist just below the thumb and see if you can feel the pulse. Another alternative is to hold your breath after the inhale and try sensing your heartbeat on the hold. The objective here is not to hold the breath at the top of the inhale other than to find your heartbeat. If you find it, see if you can feel it while inhaling and exhaling. It is common to not be able to feel it consistently throughout the entire breathing cycle at first. Just continue the count based on what you think your heart rhythm is.

f. Your mind is likely to get quite active with memories, ideas, feelings, colors or pictures. Don't try to push them away but keep your attention on counting your inhale and exhale while staying centered in the heart.

2. Expand your vocabulary of greatness qualities. On the following page is a list of positive adjectives to experiment with. Try picking a few new words a day and see if you can find evidence for them in yourself or your children/students. Try to see specific things the child is doing to illustrate the quality. No b.s.! Kids have a strong built-in "b.s. meter" and they know when something is not genuine or true.

3. Take some time to review your intentions for the children in your life from Week One. You can think of this as values clarification as well. Rework the list if necessary with insights that may have come to you from working in your heart these past weeks. Here are a few examples to spark possibilities: effort is required - perfection is not, gratitude increases happiness, mistakes help us grow, learning is life-long, challenges make us stronger, kindness, making a difference in the world starts with us, being and relishing in our uniqueness.

4. Consciously commit to using your words to see and call forth these qualities and values you have identified **in yourself**. Look for what you want to see in the children in yourself. This will strengthen your authenticity when you can see yourself being what you want to see in the children. It will supercharge your success.

100 GREATNESS WORDS

- Adaptable
- Adventurous
- Affectionate
- Agreeable
- Alert
- Ambitious
- Amiable
- Astute
- Attentive
- Authentic
- Aware
- Awesome
- Bold
- Brave
- Calm
- Capable
- Caring
- Gracious
- Happy
- Hardworking
- Honest

- Compassionate
- Confident
- Considerate
- Consistent
- Courageous
- Courteous
- Curious
- Decisive
- Dependable
- Determined
- Dexterous
- Diligent
- Diplomatic
- Dynamic
- Earnest
- Encouraging
- Energetic
- Merry
- Motivated
- Motivational
- Nurturing

- Engaging
- Enthusiastic
- Fair
- Fearless
- Flexible
- Focused
- Forgiving
- Forthright
- Free-spirited
- Friendly
- Fun
- Fun-loving
- Generous
- Gentle
- Genuine
- Giving
- Graceful
- Radiant
- Realistic
- Reflective
- Reliable

- Hopeful
- Humble
- Humorous
- Idealistic
- Imaginative
- Innovative
- Insightful
- Intuitive
- Inventive
- Joyful
- Just
- Kind
- Lively
- Loving
- Loyal
- Observant
- Open
- Open-hearted
- Open-minded
- Optimistic
- Organized
- Outgoing
- Patient
- Persistent
- Playful
- Positive
- Precise
- Punctual
- Purposeful
- Quick-witted
- Resourceful
- Sincere
- Sociable
- Social
- Strong
- Sympathetic
- Trusting
- Trustworthy
- Upbeat
- Vivacious
- Warm
- Welcoming
- Wise
- Zany

ACTIVITIES WITH THE KIDS

1. If you are a teacher, add new greatness words to your spelling list for the week and challenge the children to see these qualities in themselves and their peers.

2. If you are a parent, pick a few greatness words each day and challenge your children to see these qualities in themselves, their friends, their siblings or their parents.

WEEK SEVEN: PUTTING IT ALL TOGETHER IN THE GREATNESS CHAIR.

**CONGRATULATIONS!!
WE ARE READY FOR THE GREATNESS CHAIR!!!**

Read *The Greatness Chair* to the class or your children.

"We are all One. The beauty in one person is shared by all. The life path of one individual blesses everyone. The expression of Life neither originates within a single human, belongs to that person, nor remains within the personal boundary. Life is energy and as such, it belongs to all, reaches all, and blesses all."

– Donna Goodard

The above quote by American author Donna Goodard describes the bounty which comes from the recognition that we all share in life's energy and are not separate. When we find the beauty in ourselves and others, it blesses us all. Remember I said this was a parenting/teaching approach that was different because we are talking about energy - harnessing it, magnifying it and directing it to bring out the best in those around us by using our power of our hearts. No parenting or teaching strategy devoid of the heart's energy will bring about the transformation we seek in ourselves and our children. Practicing the exercises in this book will put you on the path of becoming an expert of your own heart's energy.

The Greatness Chair brings together all of the six powers we have discussed in this book - intention, attention, sensation, inspiration, posture and invocation - in order to bring forth the beautiful qualities we wish to see in ourselves and others. Here is a secret - you can't see a greatness in the child without already possessing the same greatness in yourself. We can only reflect what we know, even if it is not yet fully developed in us. If you can truly see it in another, trust that it is also somewhere inside of you.

Working through the weekly exercises has given you an experience of these powers. You can do the Greatness Chair activity without knowing all of this, but when you master the six powers, your influence and impact will be maximized. I liken this to understanding how to operate a boat's sails so you can reach your desired destination rather than just allowing the wind and currents to carry it in the general direction.

Let me give you a concrete example. Most of us have an expectation that children will master emotionally-intelligent social interactions by learning restraint and patience, which behaviorally, looks like avoiding interrupting and waiting their turn to speak. If we can create that outcome while simultaneously acknowledging the excitement and enthusiasm or the friendliness of the child who interrupts, we show the child their greatness at the same time. This is so much more than getting a child to behave and follow the rules! When a child sees their greatness qualities, there is a greater buy-in to following rules because they feel seen. They have a stronger and healthier connection to the parent or teacher who sees and appreciates who they are.

The basic principles to implement the Greatness Chair are listed below.

THE RULES

1. We focus on what is going right while the child is in the Greatness Chair. We can reflect on what we see in this moment or comment on something we noticed previously.

2. We do our best to use emotionally nutritious vocabulary so we can minimize anemic praise like "good job".

3. We do our best to speak heart-to-heart. We want it to land in the child's heart. You will be able to tell when this happens, I promise. The child will enter the green zone of social connection and may smile, sigh or just appear relaxed.

4. We can use our words to reflect the greatness we see, or we can ask the child to self-reflect and come up with their own attributions of greatness.

5. We commit to not leaking any negativity while the child is in the chair. We reset ourselves to only noticing what is going right. For example, if you ask a child to tell you about their greatness and they say they don't know or just get quiet, you can comment on their clarity and honesty about not knowing the answer. Or you can comment on a prolonged silence with, "I notice you are trying to answer the question. That shows your cooperation and effort."

I will suggest a few different approaches for implementation of the Greatness Chair in the activities section of this chapter, but I am confident that the greatness of your creativity will shine forth as you figure out what works best for your particular children or students.

ACTIVITIES FOR YOU

1. Practice heart rhythm meditation daily for a minimum of ten minutes. Make this commitment to yourself to honor your need for self-care and connection to your own heart, while energizing the battery to keep you full of optimism and perseverance so you can keep going as the best version of yourself as parent or teacher. Picking a specific time and place helps solidify the habit. Most people find that first thing in the morning is a time of peace and quiet before daily responsibilities begin.

2. Commit to daily use of the Greatness Chair. Just like meditation, having a specific place, chair and time adds the structure that helps successful implementation. Children thrive on regularity, predictability and daily rhythm and so do we! The instructions for how to implement the Greatness Chair are outlined below in the section, "Activities with Kids".

ACTIVITIES WITH THE KIDS

1. **Read *The Greatness Chair* to the children.**

2. Pick a time, place and chair for daily practice of the Greatness Chair. You can choose an ordinary or special chair. You can add a label or special fabric to designate it as The Greatness Chair. It is important that the children know this is a special chair and ONLY used for the Greatness Chair activity.

3. Ask the child to sit in the chair and tell you about their greatness. It can be something about themselves in general or something from a specific situation that happened that day. Or if you have chosen a word to focus on for the day, like "courage", you can ask the child to tell you when they showed courage. Some children readily tell you about their greatness and others need more mirroring and guidance. For children who need help, point out the greatness you saw during the day and then try asking the child again for their own reflections. In the beginning, children tend to tell you about their accomplishments. Help them dig deeper and ask them what qualities it took to do well. Some possibilities might be focus, preparation, perseverance, desire to please the teacher or desire to excel.

4. When the children name a greatness about themselves, reinforce it by mirroring their words back to them with your voice. This will strengthen the experience since the child will know you were listening and will feel the truth of their greatness more strongly when they hear it from a trusted adult.

5. When you call out a greatness quality in the child, try to be specific and use emotionally nutritious words with your heart's voice. If you find it hard to come up

with the right words, take a brief reset, breathe into your heart and let the words flow out without judgment. It may take a few attempts for the heart's voice to speak, and it is fine to keep talking and fine-tune it as you go. When we lecture our children for wrongdoings, we have plenty of words and can speak endlessly! If you find yourself rambling on and on in your efforts to express greatness, that is perfectly fine since the child will feel the energetic investment and attention as a display of love. In my experience, the words needed to penetrate the heart of the child eventually come out if I am patient and give myself permission to fumble around and trust the process.

Some children will reject your efforts to see their greatness. If that happens, try to notice something they cannot argue with or refute like, "I noticed you are listening to me right now and sitting in the chair. That shows me your willingness to try even though this is hard for you right now." Another way to call out greatness is to point out what is NOT HAPPENING. For example, "You could be refusing to sit in the chair and running around the room, but you aren't doing that. You are sitting still and listening. Thank you for showing me your curiosity about this activity."

6. Have FUN!! If in doubt about what to do or say, internally call out your greatness in showing up and trying and trust that your heart will never lead you astray. The Greatness Chair is a simple activity but it has layers. As you and the children practice, it will evolve and deepen.

7. Once the children experience the magic of the Greatness Chair, they will want to come sit in it at other times. It is up to you to decide how you want to handle that. You may want to build excitement by limiting its use or you may want to take advantage of the excitement and desire to be sitting in their greatness. The children should only use the chair with an adult at the beginning so you can

maintain the rules previously outlined in this chapter. Over time, the children might want to initiate going to the Greatness Chair by themselves but I recommend making it clear that they are only allowed to call out their greatness while sitting in the chair. Some children may come to associate the chair with a safe, comforting spot and just want to sit there. That is just fine, so acknowledge their greatness in knowing what they need and finding ways to soothe and comfort themselves. Alternatively, have the child tell you the greatness they are showing by this activity. The main principle is to only see what is going right while in the chair.

8. After you have practiced the Greatness Chair for a week or two, read *Sarah in the Greatness Chair* to expand the technique.

    S - I see or notice…

    A - What I appreciate about that is…

    R - That reveals to me…

    A - You ARE the greatness of….

    H - Breathe that into your heart

9. Following a daily routine for the Greatness Chair is a fun activity in its own right but also a stepping stone to making the activity part of normal communication. I recommend you continue using the Greatness Chair on a regular daily or weekly schedule. The child will associate the chair with a special place of inner strength.

10. Modifications for teenagers. Try the technique outlined above first. You might be surprised how they grow to appreciate a Greatness Chair even if they roll their eyes and make disparaging comments. Keep to the rules, reset your own energy and thank them for participating in whatever way they showed up. Remind them

that it is your choice to see their greatness and you will not be deterred. Just be real and speak from your heart. You can also bring your reluctant child into your heart privately during meditation and visualize the outcome you desire. Intention, and in fact, all of the six powers are great strengths no one can take away from you. Be patient. It may take months or years for older, resistant children. Everyone wants someone who never gives up on them.

WEEK EIGHT: RECAP AND NEXT STEPS

Phew! You made it! I have asked a lot of you so far in these weekly activities. Whether you did some or all of them, acknowledge your dedication to bringing out the best in yourselves and the children. The instructions and exercises I gave you could last a lifetime and I hope they will. Go back as often as needed to pick up more and more pieces. The good news is, these activities work on so many levels that any effort in this direction is impactful. You will see it in the children. They will help. As their excitement grows in being seen in their greatness, you will feel the energy of that and naturally want to keep it going. We are so attuned to the energy of each other, usually without our awareness.

Children are particularly attuned to our energy and your power as a parent or teacher within your heart, and you can direct it to get the results you want.

I asked you to believe your intentions matter and that your attention to positivity is powerful. I asked you to not leak negative energy. I asked you to look inward and become aware of your own inner emotional states. I asked you to read your own and the child's zone of nervous system regulation. Is it fight, flight, freeze or social connection? I asked you to expand your vocabulary to be able to fine-tune your observations of greatness. I asked you to trust the primacy of relationship over compliance. I asked you to believe that energy is the guiding principle for children and they will receive our energy by any means possible in order to have human connection. And finally, I asked you to believe your heart knows the way and that, with the help of the mind, it can bring out the best in ourselves and others.

The Greatness Chair and *Sarah in the Greatness Chair* are tools for building greatness. My wish is that the activities you practiced in the chair will become a natural part of the way you relate to children in general. You can then use the Greatness Chair as a special place – something to look forward to with anticipation. The child may eventually use it as a place of "time in" rather than "time out" to feel their greatness and reconnect with their inner strength. You will find the best way to use these tools in time, but remember to keep it special and stick to the rules of focusing only on what is going right while the child is in the chair.

I encourage you to continue heart rhythm meditation and delve deeper into that topic through IAM Heart, an organization dedicated to teaching this method and expanding the culture of the heart. I have added resources in the appendix which includes books and links to support you.

Here is to your greatness growing always.
Much love,
Dr. Friend

APPENDIX A

STEPS OF HEART RHYTHM MEDITATION

1. Sit in a chair with an upright posture and feet on the floor.

2. Close your eyes and become aware of your breath (conscious breath).

3. Breathe in and out of your nose, and deepen and slow the breath for a complete inhale and exhale. Use your abdominal muscles to help you squeeze all the air out (think belly button moving back to your spine) and then allow the inhale to naturally come in. Inhale fully to the top of your lungs, feeling the rib cage expand in the front, back and sides while keeping your shoulders relaxed (full breath).

4. Match the length of your inhale and exhale. Typical is a count of six or eight (rhythmic breath).

5. Feel your pulse or heartbeat.

6. Use your pulse or heartbeat as the counter for your inhalation and exhalation. You can count beats or place a phrase on the inhale or exhale with the correct number of syllables for your complete breath. Aim for eight counts or syllables in and eight out (heart rhythm meditation).

7. Eventually some of these technical details will become more automatic and allow you to enjoy one of the benefits of a conscious breath - greater access to the unconscious mind and voice of the heart.

8. Over time, heart rhythm meditation will stabilize your nervous system and strengthen vagal tone, making it easier to reset in those tough moments so you have the power to choose your responses wisely.

APPENDIX B

Social Emotional Learning (SEL) and the CASEL Framework for Schools

There is a growing emphasis on teaching social-emotional skills in the classroom. Broadly speaking, SEL is the process through which all young people and adults acquire and apply the knowledge, skills, and attitudes to: develop healthy identities, manage emotions and achieve personal and collective goals, feel and show empathy for others, establish and maintain positive relationships, and make responsible and caring decisions.

The Greatness Chair model, implemented through the lens of the six powers as outlined in this book, is in line with the basic tenets of SEL and the CASEL Framework.

The three broad domains of SEL include:

1. **Cognitive Skills:** executive functions, working memory, attention control and flexibility, inhibition and planning, as well as beliefs and attitudes that guide one's sense of self and approaches to learning and growth.

2. **Emotional Competencies:** skills that enable one to cope with frustration, recognize and manage emotions, and understand others' emotions and perspectives.

3. **Social and Interpersonal Skills:** enable one to cope with frustration, recognize and manage emotions, and understand others' emotions and perspectives.

One of the main models for organizing SEL curriculum in the school is called the CASEL Framework. It is organized into five areas for curriculum focus:

SELF-AWARENESS: The abilities to understand one's own emotions, thoughts, and values and how they influence behavior across contexts. This includes capacities to recognize one's strengths and limitations with a well-grounded sense of confidence and purpose. Examples include:

- Integrating personal and social identities
- Identifying personal, cultural, and linguistic assets
- Identifying one's emotions
- Demonstrating honesty and integrity
- Linking feelings, values, and thoughts
- Examining prejudices and biases
- Experiencing self-efficacy
- Having a growth mindset
- Developing interests and a sense of purpose

SOCIAL AWARENESS: The abilities to understand the perspectives of and empathize with others, including those from diverse backgrounds, cultures, & contexts. This includes the capacities to feel compassion for others, understand broader historical and social norms for behavior in different settings, and recognize family, school, and community resources and supports. Examples include:

- Taking others' perspectives
- Recognizing strengths in others

- Demonstrating empathy and compassion

- Showing concern for the feelings of others

- Understanding and expressing gratitude

- Identifying diverse social norms, including unjust ones

- Recognizing situational demands and opportunities

- Understanding the influences of organizations/systems of behavior

SELF-MANAGEMENT: The abilities to manage one's emotions, thoughts, and behaviors effectively in different situations and to achieve goals and aspirations. This includes the capacities to delay gratification, manage stress, feel motivation and agency to accomplish personal/collective goals. Examples include:

- Managing one's emotions

- Identifying and using stress-management strategies

- Exhibiting self-discipline and self-motivation

- Setting personal and collective goals

- Using planning and organizational skills

- Showing the courage to take initiative

- Demonstrating personal and collective agency

RELATIONSHIP SKILLS: The abilities to establish and maintain healthy and supportive relationships and to effectively navigate settings with diverse individuals and groups. This includes the capacities to communicate clearly, listen actively, cooperate, work collaboratively to problem-solve and negotiate conflict constructively, navigate settings with differing social and cultural demands and opportunities, provide leadership, and seek or offer help when needed. Examples include:

- Communicating effectively
- Developing positive relationships
- Demonstrating cultural competency
- Practicing teamwork and collaborative problem-solving
- Resolving conflicts constructively
- Resisting negative social pressure
- Showing leadership in groups
- Seeking or offering support and help when needed
- Standing up for the rights of others

RESPONSIBLE DECISION-MAKING: The abilities to make caring and constructive choices about personal behavior and social interactions across diverse situations. This includes the capacities to consider ethical standards and safety concerns, and to evaluate the benefits and consequences of various actions for personal, social, and collective well-being. Examples include:

- Demonstrating curiosity and open-mindedness
- Identifying solutions for personal and social problems
- Learning to make a reasoned judgment after analyzing information, data, facts
- Anticipating and evaluating the consequences of one's actions

- Recognizing how critical thinking skills are useful both inside and outside of school

- Reflecting on one's role to promote personal, family, and community well-being

- Evaluating personal, interpersonal, community, and institutional impacts

The Greatness Chair principles outlined in this book promote skills in all of the above domains. I believe it is applicable to all ages regardless of developmental level. Research suggests that evidenced-based SEL programs are more effective when they extend into the home. This book is geared for implementation by both parents and teachers. Although the activities are not specifically for the classroom and may require some modification by the teacher, the basic tenets hold for both parents and teachers. One of the premises of this book is to help adults open their hearts so they can see the greatness of the children in the here and now, and guide them to greater heights of personal growth in line with the child's unique gifts. Within both a sociocultural context with clear and predictable rules and values and the container of a safe, nurturing connection with the adults in their lives, children prosper and want to connect with others in healthy ways.

There are concerns in the field that not all SEL programs take developmental needs and tasks into account, and that "one size fits all" is not appropriate. Below are some of the developmental tasks divided by age that relate to SEL. **I argue that the program outlined in this book is appropriate for every age and sets up the conditions for the developmental tasks to unfold in an age-appropriate manner.**

Preschoolers' developmental tasks:

- Begin peer interaction while managing emotional arousal

- Initiate prosocial behaviors and interactions, along with friendships

- Stay connected with adults

- Understand basic emotional expressions, situations, and experiences - and ways to manage them (often with adult assistance), along with early efforts to solve interpersonal problems

- Begin to follow social rules, like taking turns

Elementary-aged children's developmental tasks:

- Form dyadic friendships and stable peer reputations

- Control aggressive impulses

- Demonstrate emotional regulation within the peer group, showing emotions in appropriate contexts

- Resolve more complex social difficulties with a flexible variety of solutions

Middle school students' developmental tasks:

- Build upon earlier understanding of others to comprehend more complex emotional situations in self and others

- Form a largely group-based identity with increasing independence from adults

- Become able to resolve conflicts within dyadic and group situations

High school students' developmental tasks:

- Achieve more mature relationships with others and emotional independence from parents and other adults (while still maintaining these relationships)

- Understand unique emotional perspectives

- Form an individuated personal identity (first group-based, then individuated)

- Acquire an articulated set of values and an ethical system to guide behavior

APPENDIX C

Dimensions of Well-Being – Richard Davidson Ph.D., et. al.

Richard Davidson, Ph.D., Professor of Psychology and Psychiatry at University of Wisconsin-Madison and the founder of the Center for Healthy Minds, and his colleagues have investigated the neural basis of emotion and studied various methods used to promote human flourishing - particularly, meditation. Based on decades of research, Davidson and colleagues have constructed a dimensional model of well-being with four basic components - **awareness, connection, insight and purpose**. Each dimension has components which line up very well with the six powers of intention, attention, sensation, posture, invocation and inspiration and the Greatness Chair concept outlined in this book.

Following each component of the Well-Being Model, I have listed the relevant power or concept from this book that fits into each category.

1. **Awareness:** attention, sensation, posture, inspiration

2. **Connection:** intention, invocation, connecting through positivity, sensation, intention, compassion and gratitude

3. **Insight:** inspiration, sensation

4. **Purpose:** invocation , intention

The dimensions of Well-Being Model, based on decades of research and distillation of numerous sources of scientific data, provides additional support for the importance and significance of the six powers taught in this book through the lens of The Greatness Chair. I was unaware of this model when I wrote this book and was delighted to discover the powerful alignment with the scientific research on well-being.

RESOURCES

1. *Living from the Heart: Heart Rhythm Meditation for Energy, Clarity, Peace, and Inner Power.* Puran and Susanna Bair. 3rd Edition. Living Heart Media, 2019.

2. *Energize your Heart in Four Dimensions.* Puran and Susanna Bair. 1st Edition, Living Heart Media, 2007.

3. *The Greatness Chair.* Kathleen Friend. Words Matter Publishing, 2019.

4. *Sarah in the Greatness Chair.* Kathleen Friend. Words Matter Publishing, 2020.

5. Institute for Applied Meditation - IAM Heart, Tucson, Arizona. www.iamheart.org.

6. *Transforming the Intense Child Workbook.* Howard Glasser, Nurtured Heart Publications, 2017.

ABOUT THE AUTHOR

Dr. Kathleen Friend, M.D. is a child psychiatrist, musician, meditation teacher, spiritual mentor, author, speaker and advanced trainer of the Nurtured Heart Approach. She is the author of two children's books based on NHA called *The Greatness Chair*, and *Sarah in the Greatness Chair*.

For the past ten years she has been involved with the Institute for Applied Meditation, which specializes in heart rhythm meditation and spiritual development. She is currently employed as a teacher and mentor for the organization. Her research interests involve the connection between heart rhythm meditation and vagal tone to promote mental and physical health.

Her other interests include music, and she has a B.A. in vocal performance. She continues to sing regularly in secular and religious settings.

For more information please visit her website: http://www.drfirend.net

www.ingramcontent.com/pod-product-compliance
Lightning Source LLC
Chambersburg PA
CBHW061109070526
44579CB00012B/187